Floral Frocks

Mid-1930s
Nancy Mitford wears a floral printed
silk afternoon dress.
National Portrait Gallery, London

Rosemary Harden
and Jo Turney

Floral Frocks

A celebration of the
floral printed dress from
1900 to the present day

Antique Collectors' Club

British Library Cataloguing-in-Publication Data
A catalogue record for this book is available from
the British Library

Publication designed and typeset by Northbank, Bath

Printed in China for the Antique Collectors' Club Ltd
Woodbridge, Suffolk

Antique Collectors' Club

Contents

Introduction

On any summer day in Britain in the last 80 years or so, it's fair to say that women of all ages, women living in towns and cities and women living in the countryside, women at home in the garden and women on holiday at the seaside frequently chose to wear a floral printed frock. This book celebrates the floral frock, a fashion style which was not only the mainstay of many women's summer wardrobes in the mid-20th century, but which was also part of the cultural and visual backdrop of many peoples' lives in this country.

Floral print never really went away in the 20th century. While there was immense change in both the production and consumption of fashion throughout the century, the use of different types and different designs of floral printed fabric for a summer day dress was fairly constant and fairly widespread in Britain from the mid-1920s.

The summer day dress has changed so much from the beginning to the end of the 20th century that it is sometimes hard to believe that it is same item of clothing, that is an all-in-one skirt and bodice. Ironically, at the beginning of the 20th century a dress wasn't one garment but two, a separate bodice and long skirt; but it was still known as a dress. From those long styles through the shorter skirts and bias-cut styles of the 1920s and 1930s, to the full skirted shirtwaisters and shift dresses of the 1950s and 1960s, the dress changed beyond recognition in the 20th century.

Just as the basic form of the dress changed throughout the 20th century so too there were fundamental changes in the nature of printed textiles, and of fabric itself. Right at the beginning of the new century a new printing technique – screen printing – was developed. It was a less labour intensive, and therefore a cheaper, way of printing fabric and immediately started to replace the traditional methods of block printing and roller printing, both of which had costly elements of hand preparation. This speeded up the process of supplying more fabric to the garment trade, with a corresponding demand for more fabric design. Screen printing wasn't universally adopted for fashion print until later in the century, but the process of changing production methods accelerated the rate of change in the nature and design of textiles.

PAGES 6/7
Early 1950s floral printed cotton shirtwaister by Sambo in Marchington Cottons, worn in 2006.
Private collection
© Colin Hawkins/Bath & North East Somerset Council

OPPOSITE PAGE **1940s**
Detail of a floral printed rayon frock.
Private collection

It was not only textile techniques that changed throughout the 20th century. There was also an accelerating and continuous development of new fabrics for fashion. At the beginning of the century print for fashion was almost exclusively restricted to cotton. This changed within the first 20 years of the new century, and by the end of the 20th century there was an immense range of synthetic fabrics for fashion producers to draw on.

The technological advances, and the corresponding economic imperative that drove these changes, also affected garment construction and making. Mass manufacture meant that clothes could be made more cheaply and in greater quantity than at any other time in history. Changes in the way that fashion was produced had a knock-on effect in the way that fashion was consumed. As more clothes were available at lower prices, potentially more people could acquire more clothes, whether that was through buying them, making them, or being given hand-me-downs.

Through all this change, women continued to choose to wear floral frocks, although they might be different styles and made of different fabrics. As such this unique style has been part of the dynamic, albeit a quiet and unassuming force, of everyday fashions in Britain in the 20th century. This book will investigate that dynamic through the examination of a collection of floral frocks and archive photographs.

The use of flowers as a motif for printed textile design is not a 20th century phenomenon. Flowers have been used as motifs for printed textiles since block printing was first used to decorate plain cloth. Flowers have a wealth of symbolic meanings, and this gives designers and artists access to an unspoken language that can be used to convey visual messages within their work. These can range from the straightforward, for example, a certain flower being connected with a particular country such as the rose with England and the daffodil with Wales, to something less tangible, but equally powerful. Roses, for example, can also be seen as symbols of romance, and indeed of hidden or latent sexuality.

Generally, flowers have an association with the feminine or with feminine sensibility (not necessarily just in women) because there is a tacit equation in our culture that says that flowers equal pretty, and pretty equals femininity. Through nebulous associations with innocence, purity, morality and timelessness, flowers too have a powerful symbolic link with a longing for the lost perfect past, for the endless summer day.

This book is about the eclectic spectrum of print techniques and styles used to create a plethora of fashionable and wearable floral printed dresses throughout the 20th century. Printed textiles have a role in the creation of fashionable garments. We aim to show through the dresses illustrated how good textile design can enhance the effect of a fashionable dress, and equally how good fashion design can give an extra dimension to a textile design.

Fashion studies frequently show and interpret garments by fashion designers as separate from those by other makers, such as ready-to-wear firms, and home and other dressmakers. We have included examples of all of these types of fashion in this study. Our aim in selecting the dresses has been to consider them first and foremost as a floral frock – does the dress, for example, show a synergy between textile design and fashion style? Not, is one type of dress better than the other because it was made in Paris in the dressmaking workroom of a couture house, rather than by a skilled dressmaker at her kitchen table with fabric bought from John Lewis.

The historical and cultural significance of floral printed dresses is inextricably linked with the lives of the women who wore them. This book will demonstrate the experience of wearing floral frocks, and allude to notions of fashionability, of femininity, of taste and personal choice, of occasion and place, and of the differences or similarities from generation to generation.

The book is organised in two parts to reflect two different approaches to the study of floral frocks in the 20th century. The first part concentrates on the golden age of the floral frock from the late 1920s to the early 1960s and examines primary source material including surviving dresses, family photographs and fashion magazines of the day. The second part draws on the same sources and interprets them using current critical thinking in fashion studies by concentrating on floral frocks from the 1960s to the 1990s.

As with everything, the more you look the more you find, and we have discovered floral frocks everywhere we have looked. We have investigated museum collections, private collections, vintage clothing stores, newspapers, fashion magazines, family photographs, fashion drawings, fashion photographs, film archives, collections of dressmaking patterns; the list goes on. In order to start to make observations and deductions about the floral frock phenomenon, we had to narrow our field.

This book is, therefore, selective; it is a deliberate sample from what was available to us, and from the directions that our initial research suggested. The study draws on important museum collections at the Harris Museum and Art Gallery in Preston and the Gallery of Costume in Manchester and, as such, makes reference to the important role that the Lancashire cotton industry had to play in the story of the floral frock in the 20th century. The collections of the Gallery of Costume in Manchester, the Victoria and Albert Museum in London and the Fashion Museum in Bath gave the study both a UK-wide and an international fashion dimension. Many of the family photographs in the study are drawn from two collections: one depicts life in Wales, and the second life in Scotland. The remainder of the photographs are drawn principally from families who lived in the south of England, all of whom (as so many families of this date) would have described themselves as working class, or upper working class.

The fact that the book is selective does, however, lead to interesting issues. First of all, it is likely that the floral frock 'sample' in this book may strike a chord with many people who will have versions of these images and these memories in their own family history. And secondly, the nature of the sample points out the omissions, and thus sets challenges for collecting floral frocks, and information about them to complete the picture. For example, what was the floral frock experience for women who were first, second or third generation immigrants to this country, from the West Indies, from the Indian sub-continent, from Africa and from Europe? And how did a diverse cultural background imprint itself on the use of floral print for fashion in Britain? This is just one of the challenges for dress historians, curators and collectors to get to grips with as we continue to work together to discover more about the phenomenon of the floral frock in the 20th century.

Above all though, this book is a celebration of a joyous summer style. As such, it is a tribute to the many textile designers and printers, fashion designers and makers who produced floral frocks in the 20th century, and to the countless women in Britain who wore them.

1940s
Detail of a floral printed rayon frock.
Private collection

PAGES 14/15 **Late 1940s**
Detail of a floral printed cotton day dress with design of large flowers against a zig-zag background.
Private collection

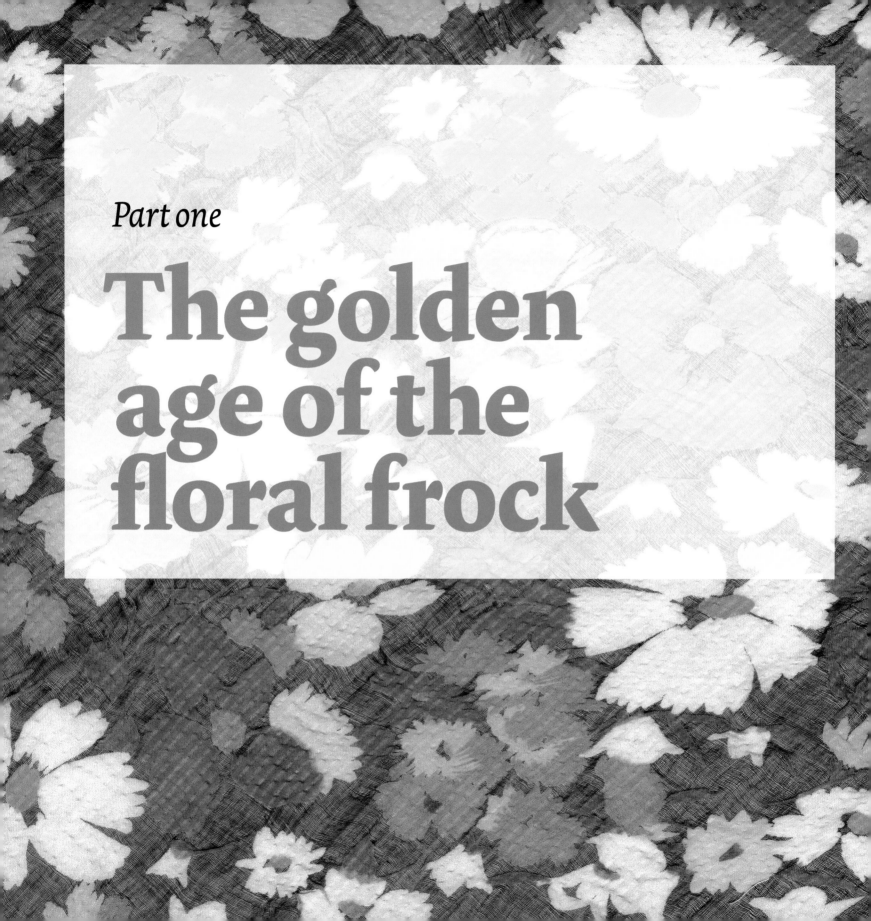

Part one

The golden age of the floral frock

The late 1920s and 1930s

Floral print was rarely seen in fashionable day wear in the early 20th century. Although there were some dresses made of floral print before the mid-1920s, they were few and far between; taken together, they do not really add up as a significant part of fashionable dress at this date. Floral print was used as a fashion fabric, but it tended to be for panels or parts of a dress, and not generally for a complete garment. It seemed that fashion designers and producers were happy to use a floral printed textile – a cheaper decorative fabric – as localised or highlight ornamentation on a dress, but not for a complete fashion look.

Linings, panels, work wear, leisure wear

By the later 1800s, garments made of fabric – generally cotton – decorated with floral print tended to be work wear, rather than high fashion. This is an association which continued well into the 20th century with women of all backgrounds wearing flowered overalls and aprons, both at work and in the home. It is true that there were some summer day dresses of floral printed cotton, and some evening dresses of floral printed silk, but these were the exceptions rather than the rule. Generally speaking, floral print was confined to more serviceable and cheaper clothes and as such was seen as a second class type of fabric.

This perception was emphasised by the fact that floral print was also used for the linings to coats, cloaks and capes in the early years of the century, giving a flash of colour and pattern which

OPPOSITE PAGE **Mid-1930s**
Detail of a floral printed silk georgette evening or full-length day dress with overall design of small flowers.
Fashion Museum

ABOVE **1922**
Panels of floral print fabric in a dress worn on holiday on the beach at Bournemouth.
Private collection

RIGHT **Mid-1920s**
A pocket on a pair of beach pyjamas made from block-printed floral cotton.
Fashion Museum

contrasted against a generally plain and frequently darker exterior. Floral print was also used for underwear and nightwear, something which like overalls and aprons continued well into the 20th century and pretty much to the present day.

At the beginning of the 20th century floral print really was the poor relation, fine for cheaper clothes, but not something that fashion designers really wished to use for mainstream fashionable summer clothes. But floral print's fortunes were about to change; and this may have been because the fabric was used in a new type of clothing, fashions for beach and for leisure activities. During the 1920s the increased emphasis on leisure and the outdoors meant that new clothes were developed for new activities, such as spending time on the beach, for example. Loose-fitting ensembles, comprising a tunic or jacket and a pair of trousers (one of the earliest occurrences of women in trousers), often known as beach pyjamas, became fashionable summer wear. Many pairs of beach pyjamas were made of woven and embroidered fabrics incorporating floral motifs; a number were also made of floral printed fabric.

Is it co-incidental that at about the same time that floral print was being used for new fashion garments such as beach pyjamas and leisure wear, it also started to be used as a fabric for fashionable day wear? The use of floral print for beachwear must, at least, have raised its profile as a fashion fabric and caused designers to look again at floral print and to re-evaluate its use.

Mid-1920s
Charlotte wears an early example of a floral frock with a bold pattern of large flowers on dark fabric at her home in Calne, Wiltshire.
Private collection

Floral frocks first start to appear in family photographs around about the mid-1920s; there are significant, although not sizeable, numbers of floral print summer day dresses of the same date in museum collections. Both photographs and dresses show an unexpectedly bold and not in the least half-hearted use of floral print. For example, the dark ground and strong yellow and orange daisy heads of the long sleeved dress from the Fashion Museum collection in Bath is not a dress for a shrinking violet. Dresses like these unequivocally announced the arrival of a new player on the fashion stage. The floral frock had arrived.

ABOVE **Mid-1920s**
Two friends dressed up for a day out;
one wears a floral print two-piece.
Fashion Museum

LEFT **Mid-1920s**
Silk georgette day dress with floral print
of large yellow and orange flowers.
Fashion Museum

Boom and bust

British society during the 1920s and 1930s is retrospectively characterised as an era of boom and slump. This terminology encapsulates geographical disparity which can be understood as a north/south divide. It also highlights the impact and effects of mass industrialisation and consumerism. Economic prosperity in the south of England, characterised by the 'boom' element, emerged as a result of new and 'clean' industry. This included the manufacture of 'white' domestic goods and appliances, new clerical positions and expansions in retail employment. On the other hand, the north of England was characterised by a decline in traditional industry such as shipbuilding, iron and steel manufacture and textiles. Whilst employment flourished in the south, unemployment and economic decline clouded the prospects of the north.

The new economic prosperity in the south offered new work opportunities for a greater percentage of the population, including women. Increased wages and access to them, along with the production of more consumer goods fuelling increased domestic consumption, enabled a buoyant economy to further flourish.

Women working

Many women in the 1920s and 1930s expected to work before they were married. Women also chose to undertake training – to be a teacher, for example – in order to have a professional career.

While there were some bold uses of floral print in the 1920s, photographs do show that at this date too there were less confident moves towards the use of floral print which resulted in less successful dresses. Perhaps this can be explained by the fact that this was a time of transition for floral print, with the fabric changing from just being a featured highlight in panels and collars to being used for a whole dress. It might also have something to do with the questionable quality of many of the synthetic fabrics, the so-called 'art-silks' which were used for floral print at this date. Art-silks were relatively cheap and therefore within the means of the younger working girl, or student teacher.

The less successful floral print dresses of the 1920s might also be attributed to the fact that the 1920s was a time of searching for a new style for fashion. Fabrics with more give, such as jersey knits, were being adopted whole-heartedly; but the quality of cut and finish differed between dresses made by couturiers in Paris, high-class dress establishments in London and the many dressmakers and fashion retailers throughout Britain. With a new fabric for summer day dresses and a new style in fashion generally, there was bound to be some experimentation, some hits and some misses. In terms of floral frocks in the 1920s this does mean that there were some inelegant and un-shapely dresses, as women and fashion producers struggled to work with and to embrace the new fashions.

Summer 1927
The girl in the centre of this group of student teachers wears a sleeveless floral print dress. It looks rather droopy, which suggests that it was made of rayon or 'art-silk'.
Private collection

ABOVE **Summer 1927**
Both tutors and students at Southlands
College in London choose floral frocks
for the end of year photograph.
Private collection

RIGHT **August 1931**
It's difficult to tell, but the dress of one
of the girls in this office in Swindon,
Wiltshire looks like a small floral
sprigged print.
Private collection

By the 1930s though, the floral frock was well and truly established. The more sinuous line – and the greater expanse of fabric – of 1930s day dresses seemed to suit floral print. This was the decade where floral frocks really came into their own as fashionable summer day wear. Women working in offices, for example, needed an appropriate type of dress, a style which was not quite best, but which was not quite workaday. A smart floral print summer day dress, frequently with a darker ground and frequently with long sleeves, fitted the bill perfectly, and can be seen often in photographs of the time.

Fashion industry

While some designers in Paris had used floral print in the 1920s, it wasn't really until the 1930s that floral print was seen again and again in dresses produced by the French couturiers. Amongst the many couture designers, elegant day dresses by the house of Paquin made of silks printed with delicately drawn flowers were frequently illustrated in British and French fashion magazines. During the 1930s it was more usual to see illustrations rather than photographs in magazines to give information about new fashions.

Representatives from the large firms that produced dressmaking patterns, such as the Vogue Pattern Service of the Condé Nast Publications Ltd, had an arrangement with the couture houses. They used the new fashions that were shown as inspir-

July 1933
Two floral frocks illustrated in *Vogue Pattern Book* with the caption 'Summer chic can be cool and crisp'.
Vogue © The Condé Nast Publications Ltd

ation for the many dressmaking patterns they sold. At this date not only did many women make their own clothes, but many others would have a dressmaker who made clothes for them. Magazines like *Vogue Pattern Book*, issued every two months, would be important ways of conveying new information about fashion styles and fashion fabrics to women throughout Britain.

Women also bought their dresses from high street shops. Most of the larger department stores had workrooms where they produced fashion garments inspired by the new styles and new styles in textiles coming from Paris. Many towns and cities had a department store, but the major stores were in London, names like Marshall & Snelgrove, Swan and Edgar and Peter Robinson. Women who didn't live in London could still buy their clothes from these larger department stores through the mail order system, with details published in newspapers and magazines, and in their in-house catalogues.

Late 1930s
Artificial silk evening dress with a
design of bunches of flowers set against
a grid background. The dress is by
Marshall & Snelgrove.
Fashion Museum

Leisure

With more people taking advantage of more opportunities for work in the 1930s, there was a corresponding and increased emphasis on opportunities for activities away from work. There was a new phenomenon in peoples' lives at this time – leisure time.

The introduction of paid holidays (in the 1920s approximately 1.5 million people in Britain received paid holidays; by 1939 this had increased to in excess of 11 million) had enabled more people to, literally, distance themselves from the world of paid work. The significance of this development, in addition to a general public concern about good health and better access and availability of public transport, manifested itself in a variety of ways, including the development of the holiday camp (Butlins opened its first camp in 1937), the development and popularity of 18th and 19th century seaside resorts such as Blackpool and Brighton, and the drive towards domestic mass tourism represented in posters, brochures and advertising campaigns of the period.

The quest for a healthy nation through the promotion of 'healthy' and 'outdoor' leisure pursuits, indicative of a society determined to recover from the casualty of war and rebuild the population, saw moves such as the development of the Youth Hostel Association founded in 1930, and the increased popularity of the Ramblers' Association. The Woman's League of Health and Beauty was also founded in 1930 and lidos, health centres and other clubs, groups and organisations directly related to health and leisure sprang up throughout Britain. The political impetus to 'get healthy' was driven by the desire to recreate a strong nation, yet the personal motivation was largely a response to the lure of leisure itself. People wanted to escape the mundane world of work and the stresses of modern urban life.

The desire to interpret leisure as an active form of escape and as a distancing from work was not only communicated in the choice of pursuit undertaken during holiday and weekend periods, but also through clothing choices. Active pursuits require suitable clothing, and mass leisure fuelled a market for leisure-wear, more casual and flexible items that would respond to the demands of more active lifestyles. Such developments are indicative of clothing distinctions that extend beyond 'Sunday Best' and work wear, firmly establishing the notion of leisure and associated activities which required specific or alternative attire. In turn this fuelled more clothing consumption across a wider proportion of the population.

Other than the development of specific 'leisure' clothing, the impact of leisure on clothing styles and designs in relation to the cultural meaning of leisure and what it represented was expressed in womenswear in a variety of ways. Initially, this can be understood in terms of 'escapism' in general, that is a distancing from the everyday and the routine.

Mid-1920s
Only the older woman in this group
having a picnic on the beach wears
a floral print frock.
Private collection

ABOVE **Mid-1930s**
Ellen wears a floral frock, which she made herself, on a British Legion outing to Portsmouth.
Private collection

LEFT **June 1930**
Knitted bathing costumes for the men, and a floral frock for one of the women during this day out to Southbrook lido.
Private collection

If the majority of the population undertaking outdoor pursuits were urban dwellers, a distancing from the everyday can be demonstrated through a return to a natural aesthetic, for example floral design. As a desire to escape to the countryside and the coast gained momentum, so did the popularity of floral prints, particularly in dresses as these garments were most closely associated with 'Sunday Best', good clothes traditionally worn on special occasions and Sundays. The floral printed dress became a mainstay of the working class wardrobe and acted as an expression of respectability or the Sunday Best let loose on holiday which represented freedom from work.

Floral frocks can be seen in the 'escape to the coast' from time to time in the 1920s, but not in significant quantities. In any case, they were generally worn by older women in family photographs of the 1920s while younger women tended to wear plain or self-coloured dresses. By the early 1930s, however, there was a change. Photographs from this date do show women on holiday at the seaside and at the coast wearing floral frocks. While in some cases the dresses might look as though they were older dresses, perhaps bought or made in the 1920s, more often than not photographs of women at the seaside show smarter day dresses, which could be described as best dresses.

Floral frocks were also worn as best dresses on days out or excursions, another aspect of the popularity for leisure pursuits.

A day out needn't necessarily mean travelling far from your home. Part of the increase of leisure in the 1930s included activities such as swimming, or visiting one of the new lidos with friends. And for these more home-based leisure activities which didn't necessarily call for a best dress, the floral frock was acceptable wear. In this way the floral frock became more and more established as everyday summer day wear for women of all backgrounds throughout the 1930s.

1933
Two girls on holiday near Lands End, Cornwall wear floral frocks that look as though they were bought or made in the 1920s.
Private collection

One of the reasons for the floral frock's successful and almost universal adoption in the 1930s was its versatility. A floral frock was smart enough to wear on excursions and days out. It was also practical enough and neither inappropriate or immodest in which to paddle in the sea. It was a style too that spanned the generations with both young and older women choosing to wear floral frocks for summers days out, whatever the occasion and whatever the activity.

Family photographs showing women wearing floral frocks have a significance and importance beyond the merely documentary or representational; the images are also bound up with our individual and collective memories of the past. The chances are that the family photograph collections and albums of many people in Britain will show women of different generations wearing floral frocks throughout the period from the early 1930s to the early 1960s. Photographs taken on days out or at birthday parties or during a visit from relatives and friends, or in a new family home or sometimes at weddings, will all very often include a floral frock.

These are the sort of special occasions when people take photographs. A camera was a luxury item for many, but if families did have access to a camera in the 1930s it was most likely (in the days before flash photography) that the photos would be taken outdoors. Photographs that were taken outside and which included people tended to be taken in the good weather, in the summer.

ABOVE **1933**
A floral frock with large single flowers worn on holiday in Newquay, Cornwall.
Private collection

LEFT **Late 1920s**
Detail of a floral printed silk georgette day or evening dress with a design of groups of flowers in a diamond trellis pattern.
Fashion Museum

The likelihood, therefore, of a family photograph including a floral frock is quite high. However, the floral frock in a family photograph is not just an historical source, but has a validity in itself. The images have a particular poignancy, and are a powerful way to evoke the past whether that is a personal or a more general past.

Floral frocks were seen both in quiet family moments at home, and for big public family occasions like weddings. Wedding dress for both brides and guests at this date mirror both fashionable day wear and fashionable evening wear. Photographs in the 1930s show guests at weddings wearing floral frocks in both day and evening styles.

By the end of the 1930s floral frocks were firmly and uniquely established as fashionable day and evening wear throughout the population. Floral frocks were worn by women who didn't work and by women who did, by women who didn't look after their own children (leaving it to nannies) and by women who did, by women who didn't have a lot of money to spend on clothes and by those who did. With the world changing in the second half of the 1930s, how would the floral frock fare in the coming decade?

OPPOSITE LEFT **Mid-1930s**
Two women of different backgrounds,
but they wear similarly patterned floral
day dresses.
Private collection
National Portrait Gallery, London

OPPOSITE RIGHT **Mid-1930s**
A floral evening dress with a dense
all-over pattern of abstract flowers.
The fabric is an early polyester and
nylon mix in a seersucker weave.
Fashion Museum

Mid-1930s
Guests at a Scottish wedding,
including one of the bridesmaids,
wear floral frocks.
Fashion Museum

PAGES 30-31 **July 1935**
Guests at a banquet at the Dorchester
Hotel, London to celebrate the Charter
Jubilee of the Institute of Chemistry
of Great Britain and Ireland. Some of
the women wear floral frocks.
Fashion Museum

29

The 1940s

The 1940s is a decade of two halves as far as fashion history in Britain is concerned, although fashion never divides as neatly as the phrase suggests. In the first half of the 1940s, the Second World War had an immediate and direct effect on fashion, but there was a different look and feel to clothes at the end of the decade; and this can be explained or interpreted as a result of living through and moving away from the dark days of the war. Through it all the floral frock had a part to play, and can be used as an example of how fashion went into hibernation in the first half of the 1940s, but emerged in a new form in the later 1940s.

OPPOSITE PAGE **1940s**
Detail of floral printed rayon sundress with an all-over design of small and larger flowers, which seem to merge into one another.
Private collection

1940s
Ada wears a floral frock while her sisters Lucy and Elsie choose plain dresses for this portrait photograph taken in Malmesbury, Wiltshire.
Fashion Museum

The Second World War

War was declared in Britain on the morning of Sunday 3 September 1939. Minutes after Prime Minister Neville Chamberlain's wireless broadcast to the nation, air raid sirens sounded in major cities, sending people running for the cellar, the Public Shelter or the hastily-erected Anderson air raid shelter in the back garden. Immediately, the war had come right into people's homes; this was to be the situation too in terms of fashion and clothing for the whole of the time of conflict. The knock-on effects of the Second World War on fashion continued well into the late 1940s, and arguably beyond.

September 1941
Two floral frocks worn for a walk on the beach with the dog at Porthcawl in Wales. A cardigan, or sometimes a coat over a floral frock, seems to have been standard British summer wear for years. The barbed wire in the background of the photographs was a precaution against enemy invasion.
Private collection

Fashion stops

In the spring before war broke out, *Vogue* fashion magazine reported on the London collections, noting that several couturiers were showing suits rather than dresses:

'These soft suits are a fashion on the incoming tide and one which threatens to swamp your floral-patterned crepe de Chine frock...'.

Vogue March 1939

It looked as though the popularity of the floral printed dress, which had enjoyed a long run through the 1930s as fashionable day and evening wear for many women, might be coming to an end, as far as the fashion industry was concerned. London was following the lead of the Paris couturiers, many of whom had also shown shorter jackets and softer suits, rather than floral frocks, for day wear.

Paris was at this time the centre of the fashion world. New ideas and changes in style came from French couturiers, and were then interpreted by dressmakers and couturiers in Britain. However, in April 1940 Paris was occupied by the German army. Although the Chambre Syndicale de la Couture (the body that governed the French fashion industry) tried to keep the couture going, none of the buyers from the major fashion stores in Europe or America or the fashion editors, or the wholesale fashion firms came to Paris to see the collections, such as they were. So, while the couture continued, albeit in a pared down state, the flow of ideas and goods stopped short, meaning that the pre-war fashion system collapsed. The mainstream fashion development of the floral frock as advocated by the fashion industry was therefore stopped in its tracks.

In Britain, in any case, the raw materials and the labour to create fashionable dress just weren't available. The clothing and textiles industries were being pushed by the Government towards production for export in an attempt to earn money for the country to pay for the war. This resulted in less clothing and textiles for the domestic market.

The Government continued the squeeze on the textile and garment trade in 1942 with the launch of the Utility scheme, a series of stringent specifications, again designed to save valuable and scarce material and resources. Journalist Anne Scott James detailed some of the earliest Utility restrictions for day dresses:

'By the latest set of regulations, no dress may have more than two pockets, more than five buttons, more than two inverted box pleats or four knife pleats, more than 160 inches of stitching, any tucks except for fullness, any ornamental stitching, any embroidery, appliqué, braid, quilting, beading, sequins, drawn thread work, a tiered skirt, epaulettes, capes, turn back cuffs, imitation pockets, buttons for ornaments or more than 2 inches of turned up hem'.

Picture Post August 1942

May 1943
Women working at Llandaff North
First Aid Post in Wales wear floral
frocks beneath their coats and overalls.
Private collection

Clothes Rationing

A year earlier, on 1 June 1941, the Government had introduced clothes rationing. This set a limit on the amount of new clothes that the civilian population could buy, and therefore that the textile and garment industry had to produce. Each person was issued with a clothes ration book containing a fixed number of coupons (66 per year when the scheme started). When buying clothes people had to surrender coupons for specific garments; seven coupons were needed for a dress.

But despite the lack of clear fashion direction from Paris, despite the Utility restrictions and despite clothes rationing, women still wanted to look fashionable and to take pride in what they wore. Where did the floral printed dress fit in with this desire to be stylish in the war years?

Make Do and Mend

All the normal routes to fashion advice and fashionable dress were closed down. This threw women back on common sense attitudes and practical skills, qualities and aptitudes that women of all classes had employed in varying degrees for years, either through choice or through stark necessity. What happened was that women made do with the clothes they had, making a dress last for years. They swapped clothes, wearing second, or even third-hand garments. They adapted and mended clothes, and they made new garments from old and worn out clothes. Al-though women were already doing this in the early years of the war, the practice was given official status with the Government's launch in 1943 of the Make Do and Mend campaign:

'The Board of Trade Make Do and Mend campaign is intended to help you get the last possible ounce of wear out of all your clothes'.

April 1943

Government booklets and magazines were full of advice on how to get new from old. One of the most often quoted ways of getting round clothing and textile restrictions and of using practical skills was to make dresses from furnishing fabric.

'We didn't feel we went without anything in the war. I had a spinster aunt who didn't spend much money on clothes. She'd come and visit my mother at our grocery shop in Skewen once a year and bring her clothing coupons. My mother would give her tea, or butter, or whatever she wanted in exchange. And so my sister, who was very fashion conscious... and all of us used to make our own clothes... so my mother had extra coupons. You could also buy curtain material with coupons... you could buy more curtain material than you could dress material. So we used to wear dresses made of curtain material... brocade, anything... we made our own clothes. It was amazing how we got by'.

Viola, *WW2 People's War* January 2006

August 1940. May 1939
A floral frock had to do summer after summer during war-time. Often this was a dress made or bought before the war. Lottie (left) made the dress that she wears here to visit her children, who had been evacuated to Devon in 1938. Mary (right) wears a dress here in the garden of her home in Surrey in the summer before the war; she still had the dress six years later when the family went on holiday to Dorset.
Private collections

OPPOSITE PAGE **1940s**
Detail of floral printed cotton shirt-waister with all-over design of small flowers interspersed with larger blue flowers.
Private collection

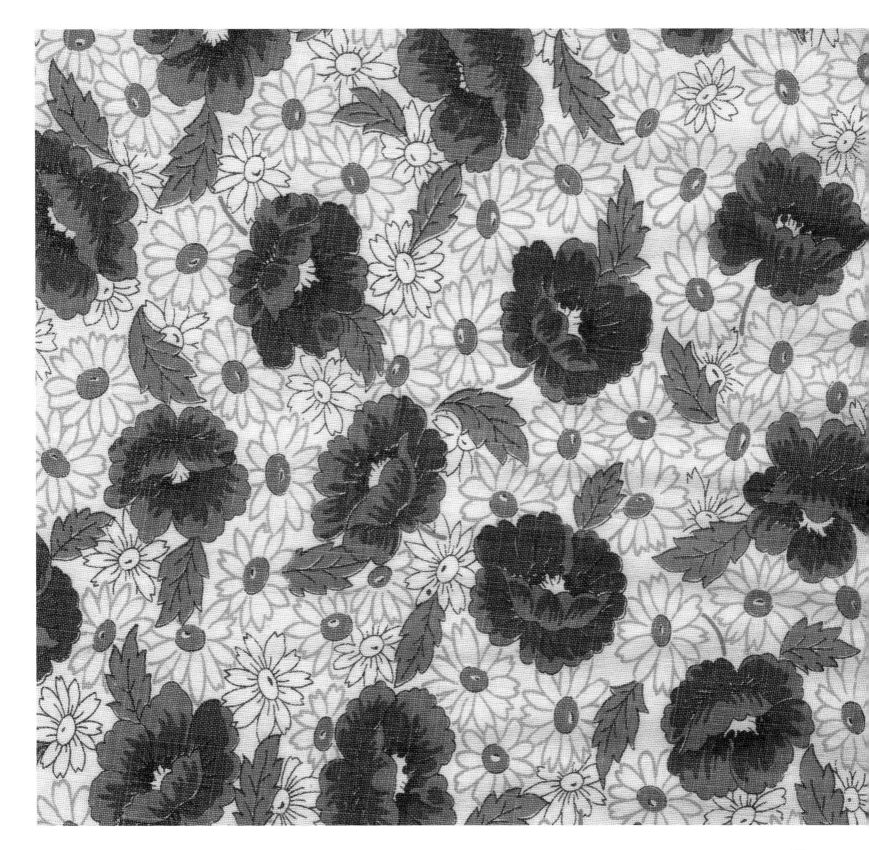

37

OPPOSITE PAGE **July 1941**
This pleated rayon crepe floral frock
by Elizabeth Henry was featured in
the Bargain of the Month section of
Vogue fashion magazine. The dress was
described as 'a classic flowered print,
which will see you through the summer
of the war, and prove a standby for
wintry afternoon occasions as well,
cost 5 guineas'.
© Lee Miller Archives, England 2007.
All rights reserved

38

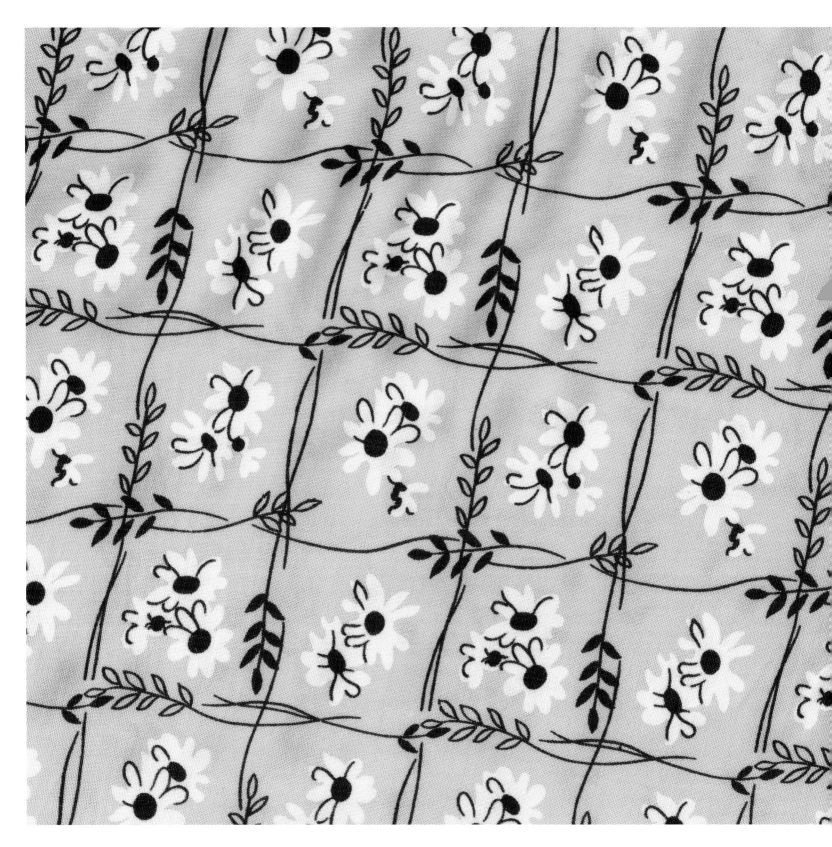

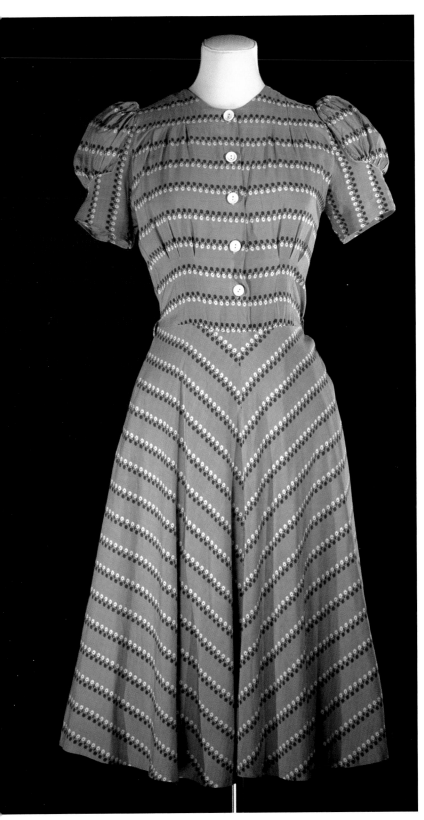

Shirtwaisters – summer day dresses with short sleeves, a centre front fastening, buttons to the waist and a belt – are sometimes difficult to date. The two shirtwaisters illustrated here look as though they were made of a furnishing fabric (perhaps yardage used for kitchen or bathroom curtains), although in fact one is made of artificial silk and the other of rayon. Both dresses may date from the latter part of the 1940s. However, the use of the soft fabric in the yellow dress particularly, which could also be used to make softly draping curtains, does make you think of all the dresses (which were eventually worn out and therefore do not survive) made by women from their old kitchen curtains during the Second World War.

'No trimmings'

The list of details that were not permitted on Utility dresses included:

> 'no ornamental stitching, any embroidery, appliqué, braid, quilting, beading, sequins, drawn thread work'.

This lack of any ornamentation on dresses, including printed pattern, is marked in fashions during the war years. Fashion photographs and descriptions of dresses featured in *Vogue* during the Second World War include virtually no printed dresses, let alone floral printed dresses. One of the only references to a floral printed dress in the magazine throughout the whole six years of the war is a line drawing by Cecil Beaton, published just before

OPPOSITE PAGE **1940s**
Detail of floral printed rayon shirt-waister with a design of groups of two or three small flowers enclosed in a grid pattern made up of stems and leaves.
Private collection

1940s
A floral frock which doesn't look like a floral frock. The stripes on this artificial silk shirtwaister by Betty Baxley Frocks are made up of two lines of small blue and white flowers.
Fashion Museum

VE day, when the war was over:

'Daisy-patterned brown rayon for a dress featuring a panel, which widens the shoulders, narrows the waist, and from which the skirt fullness radiates in unpressed pleats'.

Vogue, April 1945

However, by contrast, in *Vogue Pattern Book*, the magazine aimed at women who made their own clothes or employed a dressmaker, there were plenty of illustrations of day dresses made from floral printed fabric throughout the war years. There was advice about different styles of floral printed dress for different occasions: short sleeves and a button-up collar for the country; while three-quarter length sleeves with a V-neck was right for a day in town. These floral print details may have been an illustrative device to brighten up a plain drawing; however it could also suggest that although fashion firms might not have made dresses from floral print in the early 1940s, women at home certainly did.

Fabrics for fashion

The textiles that were available to home dressmakers were not necessarily fashion fabrics designed and produced during the war years. Indeed, just about all of the textile producers in Britain in the 1940s were re-directed towards the war effort, either making fabrics to be used in the war, such as black-out fabric, or textiles for export. There was little production of printed fashion fabrics for the home market.

Furnishing fabrics could be used for dressmaking, although the production of furnishing fabrics was also curtailed during the Second World War. It's likely too that women used fabrics that had been produced before the war, and which had perhaps remained unsold in haberdashers and other shops. The fashion floral prints of the 1930s were exuberant and confident designs often with dense and most frequently all-over patterns of flowers on a dark or light coloured ground. Illustrations in magazines and family photographs of women in the war years do show this kind of floral print.

Once the war was over the situation didn't immediately change as there was still rationing and shortages, but new fabrics started to become available. For the first time for a number of years there were advertisements from fabric manufacturers, although they frequently alluded to the continuing shortages:

'Marshall Summer Fabrics… Supple rayons and crisp cottons, flower strewn… cool and sparkling with colour – or plain and fresh as a daisy… in the Marshall summer range there are fabrics to face even the vagaries of an English summer. But supplies are still very scarce'

Vogue, July 1947

An advertisement for a fashion textile called Tulip by Moygashel Fabrics at the same date emphasizes the problem faced by home dressmakers: the fabric cost 5/3, plus two coupons a yard.

August 1946
Muriel and Mary wear floral frocks on holiday at West Bay, Dorset. This is the same dress that Mary wore for the photograph in the garden of her home Surrey in May 1939.
Private collection

OPPOSITE PAGE **1940s**
Detail of rayon floral print frock with design of large and small flowers along with some leaves and seed pods.
Private collection

With the annual coupon allowance at around the equivalent of 40 a year at this date, the six or so that would be needed to buy a dress would make a big hole in the amount of coupons available for the year.

Moygashel Fabrics produced linens, the traditional fabric of Northern Ireland. From the late 1940s the firm produced a number of bold coloured floral prints, which were used by emerging British wholesale fashion firms for summer dresses. While occasionally there were floral printed dresses of linen at this date, it was more usual for floral dresses to be made of cotton or different types of synthetic fabric in the late 1940s.

Synthetics

Textile firms including DuPont in America and Courtaulds in Britain had been developing various artificial silks throughout the 1920s and 1930s. Rayon was one of the most successful of the synthetics: its characteristic luminosity gave the impression that it was silk. Rayon was used extensively for floral printed frocks in the years following the war, sometimes in a smooth satin weave, which made it particularly shiny. Rayon had been developed before the war and used extensively although sometimes not very successfully for fashion fabrics. For this reason it had a slightly cheap and tired reputation, and tended to be referred to in pejorative terms, appearing for example in features in fashion magazines for those with limited means.

1949
Detail of a floral printed viscose linen-look button-through dress by the Calico Printers' Association with a lively pattern incorporating twining stems and leaves as well as bright coloured flowers.
Gallery of Costume, Manchester City Galleries

Cotton

Although rayon and other synthetic fabrics were used for floral frocks in the later 1940s, new floral designs were also being produced in cotton fabrics. In 1940 in the early years of the war the Government sanctioned the creation of The Cotton Board, and the associated Colour Design and Style Centre, both of which were based in Manchester. The intention was that The Cotton Board would bring individual cotton manufacturers and suppliers together, to promote cotton and its use as a fashion fabric. The date at the beginning of the war is significant as the driving force must have been the need to create a body which would generate sales of British goods, principally for export.

The aim of the Colour Design and Style Centre was to seek ways in which standards of design could be improved. It also had a remit to find ways of maximising opportunities to make sales through emerging new practices, those which would today be called marketing. Although it wasn't immediately apparent, initiatives such as this did stimulate new design. Floral print benefited, and there were developments in the ways that flowers were treated as motifs in print. The new floral designs moved away from smaller blooms used in an all-over style to experimentation with bolder colours, larger motifs, and different styles of drawing and placing flowers in a printed textile design.

1948
Detail of a floral printed rayon satin evening dress with a diamond grid pattern of loose bunches of flowers. Ruby wore this dress made by Miss Ada Smart, Dressmaker, to dinners and dances in the late 1940s.
Fashion Museum

This can be seen in a collection of floral print summer day dresses produced in 1949 by the Calico Printers' Association. The CPA was a trade organisation founded in Lancashire in 1899. It celebrated its Golden Jubilee in 1949, and it seems likely that this collection was associated with the celebrations. The whole exercise underlines how during the Second World War the printers of the CPA had together produced millions of yards of material for the war effort (including 50 million discs for the inside of gas masks), but could rapidly respond to post-war circumstances, and turn to producing bold new fashion fabrics. There are 40 dresses in the collection and the CPA donated them all to the Whitworth Art Gallery in Manchester in the 1960s. The collection was subsequently transferred to the Gallery of Costume in Manchester in 1997, where it is an invaluable resource for the study of cotton as a fashion fabric in the post-war period.

The first Director of the Colour Design and Style Centre in Manchester was James Cleveland Belle, who had been a buyer for the Bon Marché department store in Liverpool. Cleveland Belle was also an adviser to Horrockses, Crewdson and Company Ltd, a cotton manufacturing firm in Preston which was founded in the late 18th century and which enjoyed a reputation for producing excellent cotton fabric, including cottons such as towels and sheeting. They were also known for their cotton nightwear, many pieces of which featured floral print. In 1946, with advice and direction from Cleveland Belle, Horrockses set up Horrockses

Late 1940s
Mavis wears a dress by Horrockses Fashions on Morecambe pier in Lancashire. This was Mavis's favourite dress, although she didn't think of it as her best dress.
Harris Museum and Art Gallery, Preston

Fashions producing ready-to-wear dresses and beachwear made from Horrockses cotton fabric. Right from the early years of the new firm, Horrockses Fashions did something different with the designs for floral print. The densely packed or straight individual drawings of flowers of the 1930s are gone; instead there are new thoughts about using more space and lines and incorporating drawn flowers in a different and modern way.

Horrockses dresses are synonymous with floral printed frocks of the 1950s, and many women have memories either of owning, or wanting to own a Horrockses floral print dress. It is interesting to note, however, that Horrockses Fashions was set up just after the war in the 1940s, not the 1950s. In the immediate post-war period in Britain the twin needs for hard cash (through export or home sales) for a country made bankrupt through war, and for colour and pattern for a weary and jaded population drove a number of new initiatives, such as the founding of this forward-looking ready-to-wear clothing firm. New moves such as this were to have an effect in the decades following the world-wide conflict.

Late 1940s
Mavis's cotton dress, by Horrockses
Fashions, with a diagonal design of
trails or garlands of flowers set against
a pattern of horizontal lines. Mavis paid
about £4 for the dress.
Harris Museum and Art Gallery, Preston

After the war

'Let's have back... lovely colours in fabrics... flowers in our flower-beds, and cabbage banished to its proper place out of sight and out of smell'.   Vogue, 1945

Women had continued to wear floral frocks throughout the war years, despite the shortages and the stagnation of fashion ideas and fashion goods. Although there were doubtless family occasions and days out during the war, there are many more family photographs from the second half of the 1940s showing women sitting in their gardens with their children and grand-children, or on days out or at the seaside. The war had meant that often families were split up and in any case people were living in difficult circumstances. Even if people did have cameras in the early 1940s, film was subject to the same kind of shortages as textiles and clothing during the war. It is noticeable how often family photographs in the later 1940s feature floral frocks, and interesting also to note how women of different generations wear different styles of floral frock. Younger women embraced the newer styles in both textile design (with changes in placing floral motifs, often more spread out and not necessarily in all-over regular patterns, but often in muted colours) and fashion design (wider skirts), while older women continued to wear either the actual dresses or the styles of their youth.

Generally speaking, family photographs tend to be taken at significant occasions, like weddings and other family get-to-

OPPOSITE PAGE **Summer 1947**
Grace and her daughter Gwen wear floral frocks sitting in the garden at home in Sutton, Surrey. Grace's dress has large single flowers while Gwen's has a smaller pattern on a softer fabric, which drapes at the bodice and sleeves.
Private collection

1940s
Floral printed cotton day dress with design of large flowers against a zig-zag background.
Private collection

gethers, or on holidays or days out. These are traditionally times when people choose to wear their best or special clothes. It is difficult therefore to draw hard and fast deductions about dress from family photographs, just because the evidence is prejudiced towards the special rather than the everyday, which is not to say that they don't have validity. However, in terms of the floral frock and its place at the end of the 1940s it seems fair to say that since these dresses appear on these 'significant' occasions, they were dresses that had special value for their wearers and which were considered to be a best day dress.

A new shape for dresses

The shape of dresses changed at the end of the 1940s. This was directly attributable to Christian Dior's famous New Look collection. It was Carmel Snow, editor of the influential American fashion magazine *Harper's Bazaar*, who christened Dior's first fashion collection, shown in Paris on 12 February 1947, the New Look. Dresses and suits in Dior's collection were characterised by the use of yards of fabric in full skirts, and by nipped-in waists, thus creating an exaggerated and curvaceous female form.

Although it was frowned on in some quarters as a scandalous waste of fabric in a world where shortages and privation were still the order of the day, there is no doubt that the New Look was embraced by women of all backgrounds throughout Britain. Some women might have had means to buy either the versions of the New Look by couture houses or fashion wholesale firms, but many women saved their coupons and their money to buy fabric to make their own versions of this brand new style.

The new fashion shape became synonymous with a new femininity, and since then has been interpreted as evidence of a post-war yearning for a utopian and nostalgic peacetime world where women were women, and men knew it. Indeed, the same fashion magazine that Carmel Snow edited had expressed this two years before she christened the New Look:

> 'This year begins a new era and it follows as the peace of war that men want women beautiful, romantic... birds of paradise instead of hurrying brown hens'.
>
> *Harper's Bazaar*, October 1945

An obvious way to create these 'birds of paradise' was to produce clothes using colourful fabrics incorporating traditional feminine motifs, such as floral print. Ironically, Christian Dior's collections at the end of the 1940s didn't include a great deal of floral print. However, the New Look and the re-discovered appreciation of the feminine, coupled with a quiet re-surgence in this country of textile design, set the scene for the continued development of the floral printed frock in the new decade.

July and August 1949
The same dresses worn on two days out to the beach in Wales in summer 1949 – Llantwit Major in July, and Tenby in August. The younger woman's dress has all the hallmarks of the new fashions in florals: a fuller skirt – courtesy of the New Look – and a more scattered treatment of floral motifs. The older woman chose checks rather than florals for her summer frock.
Private collection

OPPOSITE PAGE **Late 1940s**
Detail of a floral printed rayon day dress with a design of large blown roses against a woven or latticework background.
Fashion Museum

The 1950s and early 1960s

'The prettiest summer for years... The prettiest of wild flower colours – pinks, blues, leaf-greens, and whites, freshly with one another – blooms across the fashion summer.'

Vogue, June 1954

Floral frocks made the transition from the 1940s to the 1950s and one decade blurred into the next with styles at the beginning of the new decade still looking like those from the end of the 1940s. In some instances, the dresses that can be seen in family photographs from the early 1950s are the same dresses that women made, bought and wore in the 1940s. Rationing continued in Britain until the early 1950s, and a new decade did not mean a freedom from shortages and restrictions on the availability of new clothes.

However, there was a new mood in fashion in the early 1950s, one which can be characterised as a return to femininity. Styles with fuller skirts, emphasising a tight fitting waist and a frivolous use of fabric, demonstrated a disregard of wartime restrictions and epitomised the fashion of the early part of the decade. A search for the new, which both rejected austerity and showed a desire to recapture a mood of romance, dominated fashion design for women during the early years of the postwar period, and indeed women's perceptions of what was fashionable for a long time after. As far as floral frocks are concerned, it's fair to say that the ultra-feminine New Look shape was popular through the 1950s and arguably into the early 1960s.

OPPOSITE PAGE **Late 1940s or 1950s**
Detail of a floral printed rayon twill sleeveless day dress with a painterly design of flowers and leaves. The textile design is like a painting on a canvas.
Private collection

Early 1950s
Dancing at home wearing a sleeveless floral frock.
Fashion Museum

OPPOSITE PAGE **May 1952**
Short evening dresses were
fashionable in the 1950s. This
floral example, published in *Vogue*
and made from a *Vogue Couturier
Pattern* in flowered organdie, was
also noted as being 'pretty enough
for a summer trousseau'.
*Coffin/Vogue © The Condé Nast
Publications Ltd*

1957
A sleeveless floral frock designed by
Carven of Paris and made of ribbed
cotton produced in Manchester.
The fabric is gathered and stitched
at the waist so that the blue rosebuds
line up closely.
*Gallery of Costume, Manchester
City Galleries*

Late 1950s
Showcard advertising full-skirted
dress and bolero top by Horrockses
Fashions.
Harris Museum and Art Gallery, Preston

Early 1950s
Doris wore this sun-dress and
short-sleeved jacket by Horrockses
Fashions as a holiday dress.
It's possible that the fabric was
designed by Alistair Morton.
Harris Museum and Art Gallery, Preston

The fashion industry

The fashion system fell back into the pre-war pattern at the end of the Second World War with Paris quickly re-asserting itself as the centre of the fashion world. The Paris couturiers set the ideas about changes in style, and changes in uses of fabrics, with the rest of the world-wide fashion industry following their lead, to a greater or lesser extent. And Paris couturiers did embrace floral print in the 1950s:

> 'News from Paris – the print restored to high favour – each a leaf out of a gardener's handbook – rosebud chiffon, poppy-peppered shantung, formal leafy patterns, bright blurred flower prints...'
>
> *Vogue*

Throughout the early 1950s, Dior (the originator of the New Look) was one of the couturiers to use floral print extensively, often for elegant and classy silk day dresses, but also for evening dresses. Other Paris couture houses also used floral print for their summer day dresses. Occasionally, two couturiers would use the same textile: Givenchy and Fath, for example, used the same flower and stem patterned textile in dresses in 1952.

Representatives from Britain's numerous wholesale fashion houses – firms like Susan Small and Frank Usher – would go to see the couture collections in Paris and would pay for the right to use toiles, which they would either reproduce or use as inspiration for their own designs. Many of these firms produced floral frocks in the 1950s.

OPPOSITE PAGE **July 1954**
British ready-to-wear wholesale fashion houses produced floral print frocks for each summer during the 1950s. This day dress with its abstract floral design was by Susan Small and cost seven guineas.
Hammarskiöld/Vogue © The Condé Nast Publications Ltd

1959
A teacher bought this cotton dress by Horrockses Fashions to wear on holiday and at weekends, rather than at work. It cost £6, which was half her weekly wage.
Harris Museum and Art Gallery, Preston

There were a number of new wholesale fashion houses set up in Britain at this date, including Sambo, founded by Samuel Sherman in the late 1940s. The Sambo brand became synonymous with crisp cotton shirtwaister dresses in the 1950s, and they were frequently in floral print. Sambo, like Horrockses Fashions, relied on good quality cotton, many of which were supplied by textile producers Marchington Cottons

Home dressmaking

For most women in the 1950s it was usual to be able to sew and most had the dressmaking skills to make their own summer dresses. They worked from Butterick, Simplicity, McCall's and Vogue dressmaking patterns, or from patterns published in or available through newspapers and magazines. Home dressmakers bought the three yards or so of dress fabric, in 36 or 45 inch fabric width, from haberdashers, department stores or market stalls so as to make their own summer dresses at home on hand or treadle operated sewing machines. Making your own clothes saved money, with the difference between a shop-bought and a home-made dress being anything in the region of £4 or £5.

There were plenty of advertisements for new fabrics emphasising the advantages of home dressmaking and the virtues of the floral printed dresses of the early 1950s. In one, a model girl complete with pearls, jaunty little hat and white gloves wears a cotton dress printed with large floral clusters.

This advertisement for Marchington cottons emphasised how it was economic and labour-saving to make your own dresses from the new fabrics, and that the floral printed dress which you made from Marchington cotton would give you a dress that would be acceptable both in the day and in the evening:

'Marchington Miracle cottons in Everglaze re-value the pound. The fact is you can buy more fashion for your money nowadays, because cottons are climbing the heights, but keeping the same price tags on them. A frock of Marchington cotton in Everglaze can be silken smooth or crisply embossed. It can rustle or fall in silent folds, go to dinners, dances, cocktails or be just an everyday cotton frock that looks and goes on looking twice as good as other cotton frocks. Everglaze is a new magic that rewards cotton for its virtue by giving it more virtue – resistance to wrinkles, shrinking, spots and soil: new textures, new possibilities. And there's no lapse in the behavior of these cottons after washing. So you see high style fabrics are no longer a matter of money, but a money-saving matter.'

Vogue, April 1953

PAGES 60-61 **June 1952**
An end of year photograph at a teacher training college in Kingston, Surrey shows both students and tutors wearing floral frocks. While the patterns of the floral fabrics from which the frocks are made are varied, the styles of the dresses the younger women wear are similar.
Private collection

OPPOSITE PAGE **Early 1950s**
Floral printed cotton shirtwaister by Sambo in Marchington Cottons. The design is of realistically drawn large single flowers arranged in horizontal bands on a background scattered with just the outlines of smaller flowers.
Private collection

Different florals for different occasions

In the 1950s there were increased opportunities for different types of socialising. The floral frock had a part to play in them all; indeed, the floral frock had a number of applications, and therefore different forms throughout the 1950s. This was in contrast to the use of floral frocks in the 1940s where one dress or at least one style did for a number of uses.

The floral printed frock was standard daytime summer wear for women of all backgrounds throughout the 1950s. A floral print dress could also work on a number of different daytime occasions, as in the 1930s. It would, for example, be acceptable as a smart dress for a day out or excursion; and equally a floral print could work for more relaxed activities, on the beach for example. In many cases, it was of course the same dress, but the point is that a floral frock was not out of place or an inappropriate dress in either situation. Even if the weather was chilly or overcast as often in British summers, women still wore their floral printed frocks. They simply put on a coat or a knitted cardigan over the top.

OPPOSITE PAGE **1954**
Greta bought this cotton dress by
Horrockses Fashions in Blackpool and
wore it as a summer holiday dress. This
is another dress made of fabric with
horizontal bands of floral motifs; it was
a fashionable look at the beginning of
the 1950s. The fabric has been roller-
printed rather than screenprinted.
Harris Museum and Art Gallery, Preston

July 1952
Three women wear floral frocks – two
with knitted cardigans over the top –
on an overcast day out to Bowness in
the Lake District.
Private collection

Early 1950s
At this date the same floral frock was
acceptable both as leisure wear and as
a smart day dress. Joan's floral frock
works just as well for playing about
on the beach as it does on the coach
journey on this day trip to the seaside.
Private collection

Summer 1952
Ann, Margaret, Mary, Lilian, Pat,
June, Brenda and Mavis all wear
floral frocks on a youth club outing
to Littlehampton, Sussex.

ABOVE **December 1957**
Gwen wears a dark-coloured long
sleeved winter floral frock at the
wedding of her daughter in Cheam,
Surrey.
Private collection

LEFT **July 1953**
Constance's light-coloured floral frock
marks her out from the other guests at
her daughter's wedding near Clitheroe,
Lancashire.
Private collection

OPPOSITE LEFT **December 1957**
Detail of a floral printed polyester
base fabric with a design of large
roses merging into one another.
The design has been printed onto
the material by a transfer method.
Private collection

OPPOSITE RIGHT **1950s**
A floral frock for a family wedding
in Scotland.
Fashion Museum

Floral frocks in the 1950s were acceptable for the most formal day-time occasions, such as weddings. It was quite usual, for example, for the most important guest at a wedding, the mother of the bride, to wear a floral printed frock.

Floral frocks were advocated as day into evening wear time and again throughout the 1950s. An afternoon dress which would work through to the evening was frequent fashion advice during the 1940s when clothing was restricted. The practice seems to have become well-established in the 1950s, either through custom, continuing shortages, or a continuing and now ingrained need for economy.

> 'Atrima at all times, in summer sunshine or moonlight. This pretty team loves sunny days... and evening parties, too! Cotton piqué, it has an ad-lib bolero with tiny slit sleeves. Choose your flowers in blue, grey and yellow, or red, grey and green, or purple, grey and yellow... all on white. 5 guineas'.

Vogue, May 1953

Floral frocks were acceptable throughout the 1950s for the most formal day occasions. While some couturiers in Paris and London designed evening dresses in floral printed silk, Horrockses Fashions developed a range of evening dresses in floral printed cotton in the mid-1950s. One of these dresses, now in the collection of the Fashion Museum in Bath, and dating from 1955, has beautifully drawn yellow irises scattered across the crisp white cotton ground. The dress has a long stole lined in bright yellow cotton,

which is attached at one side to be worn around the shoulders. While it wasn't a line they continued, preferring to stay with the floral printed cotton day dress, the Horrockses Fashions experiment with evening dresses in the mid-1950s shows that it was quite acceptable to wear a printed floral cotton frock as an evening dress, something which would have been unimaginable 50 years earlier.

Despite its use for formal evening dresses, traditionally made of the grandest and most expensive textiles, floral print in the 1950s retained its use as a fabric for more marginal wear, rather than as an exclusive fashion fabric. Floral print was still used for underwear and nightclothes, as well as for aprons and overalls, and for childrens' clothes. It was still often seen in, and often suggested for, clothes to be worn on the beach, whether these were day dresses, sun dresses or for playsuits and shorts. These types of garment were often featured in the less expensive 'More Taste than Money' sections of magazines. So although floral print had come of age as a fashion fabric in the early 1930s, it still retained its association and use for non-fashion wear.

LEFT **1950s**
Despite its use a fashion fabric, floral print was still used for leisure wear, in garments such as sun-dresses and shorts.
Fashion Museum

RIGHT **1959**
Sheila made this evening dress from fabric bought in John Lewis in Oxford Street, London using a pattern by Victor Stiebel, published two years earlier in *The Daily Telegraph*.
Fashion Museum

A new age

In the early 1950s there was a new young monarch in Britain. The Coronation of Queen Elizabeth II in 1953 was heralded as the dawn of a new Elizabethan age and seen as a symbol of a brand new world. For the first time in many years, ultimate constitutional power in the country had passed to a woman, and a young woman at that. The fact that the new monarch was a woman meant that the celebrations took on an abundance of floral symbolism, and none more so than in fashion. Indeed, the dress the new young Queen wore for her coronation was covered with flowers, albeit depicted through the grander art of embroidery rather than in print.

However, floral prints were not only indicative of this new femininity, but were also linked to a new mood of hope and faith in the future. To refer to nature in motif construction can be seen as part of a desire for renewal, of lettings things run their course, of putting faith in a higher power, and sowing seeds for the future. Floral motifs and patterns here express re-birth, starting afresh, while at the same time returning to something beyond man's ultimate control.

LEFT **1950s**
New houses and new floral prints for a modern age.
Fashion Museum

RIGHT **Early 1950s**
Bright orange and yellow roses in this floral printed cotton frock by Horrockses Fashions.
V&A Images/Victoria and Albert Museum, London

Synthetics in a new age

One of the most important ways that fashion looked forward to a brand new world in the 1950s was in the development and widespread use of new synthetic textiles. Synthetics had been used as fashion fabrics since the 1920s, but it was in the 1950s that they came of age; they were embraced and used by the whole range of fashion producers, from the couturier to the home dressmaker. The creation of a number of companies and organisations in the 1940s and 1950s, such as the British Nylon Spinners and the Man Made Fibres Association, meant that synthetic fabrics and fibres were not only a significant economic force in fashion and textiles, but also had a credibility and a visibility that they hadn't previously enjoyed.

The way in which the new textiles were brought to the public's attention was also new. Month after month, week after week in magazines and newspapers, and on television, there were features and advertisements showing the delights of these new wonder fabrics. And time and again a floral frock was used to extol the virtues of the new fabrics.

> *'The Magic of Nylon. Peggy Page casts a summer spell in diaphanous gossamer Nylon, with multi-coloured flowers floating on a cloud of white. At £6 19s 6d.'* Vogue, May 1955

Nylon, developed by American firm DuPont, was the first completely synthetic fabric. It was launched in 1939, principally to be used for nylon stockings. After the war DuPont came to an

Late 1950s
Elinor wore this nylon floral print dress by Horrockses Fashions when she accompanied her husband, who worked for the firm, to London for the seasonal fashion shows.
Harris Museum and Art Gallery, Preston

arrangement with British firms ICI and Courtaulds, and nylon became one of the three main types of synthetics used for fashion fabrics in the 1950s. The others were polyesters and acetates. Terylene, developed and sold by ICI, was one of the main polyesters; Tricel, developed by British Celanese, was one of main acetates.

New treatments for textiles were also developed during the 1950s, and these too had a direct effect on the look of floral printed frocks. Glazes and coatings, for example *'Calpreta permanent glaze – ideal for summer fashions'*, were added to natural fabrics, principally cotton, and these gave the textiles a sheen and handle which they wouldn't have achieved in their natural state. This worked particularly well for cotton which went droopy after a couple of washings. It was these glazes and treatments that gave the distinctive crisp look of cotton dresses in the 1950s.

Two of the major selling points of both the synthetic fabrics and the treated fabrics were that they were crease resistant and easy to wash. It is interesting to note how often these claims were used in advertisements for fabrics and fashions. Clearly, it was something that concerned women in the 1950s and assurances on washability were therefore likely to sell more products. In an advertisement published in fashion magazines, a woman in a floral printed frock assures her husband:

'Yes dear lovely to look at – and wonderfully washable!
Anti shrink rayons and cottons – guaranteed by Grafton.'

1958
Marjorie bought this dress at a reduced price when she worked at Horrockses in her late teens. She wore the dress to dances and on trips to Blackpool at weekends. The dress is by Horrockses Fashions and the fabric was designed by John Tullis.
Harris Museum and Art Gallery, Preston

Young women

Fashion in the 1950s was characterised by a growing awareness of youth and of the power that younger women and girls had as consumers. Fashion is a business and where there is demand so supply will follow, and many wholesale firms started lines specifically aimed at younger women in the 1950s. Horrockses Fashions, for example, launched Pirouette Fashions, which was identified in their advertising material as being fashion for teenagers. Other dress houses, such as The Linzi Line, were targeted at younger customers.

ABOVE AND OPPOSITE **1950s**
A summer holiday or day out in Scotland, and the women chose to wear circular floral print skirts or floral dresses while paddling in the sea.
Fashion Museum

LEFT **1950s**
Floral printed cotton day dress by The Linzi Line with a design of different types of single flowers all looking as though they are hanging on the horizontal lines.
Fashion Museum

1950s
Floral skirts on a picnic. The same
people as those paddling in the sea
(pages 74/75) share a picnic by the side
of a Scottish river on the same day.
Fashion Museum

Some of the dresses marketed as being for younger women and girls were made of floral print. They were all generally described with phrases like 'care-free', 'youthful and gay'.

But despite this acknowledgment of and marketing toward youth, many women in their late teens and early twenties at the end of the 1950s looked like younger versions of their mothers. On some level floral frocks helped to establish that status. It is true that there were changes of style in the floral frocks toward the end of the 1950s and into the 1960s. Rather than the shirtwaister style these dresses had plain bodices and fastened at the back with a full-length zip. Revere collars were replaced by boat or straight necklines. However, this still wasn't that different from the style that had been fashionable from at least the beginning of the 1950s, and which continued in popularity throughout the decade. So even the newer styles, dresses such as the 'Younger Set' dress by Berkertex, which were being marketed for younger women, looked by and large like the dresses that women had been wearing throughout the 1950s.

1957
A young woman wearing a more modern shaped floral frock, not unlike the Trapeze shape made famous by Yves Saint Laurent in his early collections for the house of Dior. The skirt, which is probably supported by starched or net petticoats, flares out from a high waist. This style needed a lot of fabric, perfect to show off an exuberant floral print.
Fashion Museum

This similarity in fashions for younger and older women in the 1950s is emphasised in an advertisement for John Smedley frocks in Kastoris cotton in 1954, showing two women of the same age wearing identical shirtwaister floral frocks. One frock, called 'Sally', was made of a cotton with a design of a checked grid ground over which are scattered naturalistic flowers. This was described as youthful and carefree. The second frock, 'Sandra', a similar belted style, but with a collar and in a print with strong vertical lines and Japanese-looking chrysanthemum heads, is noted as being 'more sophisticated'. Looking at the photograph today, the dresses look no different from each other. Indeed, they even cost the same price. However, perhaps the image would have been read in a different way 50 years ago, and women would have known that one was a young woman's dress while the other was for a woman of more mature years.

At the end of the 1950s and beginning of the 1960s, both mainstream textile and fashion producers were acknowledging that there were more younger women with money to spend on fashions. They were designing styles and textiles which they felt had a younger look and feel, but this was still within the confines of a basic fashion shape and style which had been around for some time; it didn't really make younger women look that much different.

OPPOSITE LEFT **Early 1960s**
Floral printed cotton day dress by Berkertex Younger Set in Tootal cotton with a design of large flowers on a white ground. The dress has small bows at the shoulders, a stylistic device intended to appeal to the younger customer.
Fashion Museum

OPPOSITE RIGHT **Early 1960s**
More youthful bows, but this time at the waist rather than the shoulders. This floral printed cotton sateen day dress with a design of similar large flowers – although these are drawn in a less realistic way – was made by a skilled dressmaker.
Fashion Museum

1954
Advertisement for John Smedley floral frocks in Kastoris cotton. Was there really any difference between dresses for older women and dresses for younger women in the 1950s?

There was a new breed of fashion designers, however, in the late 1950s and early 1960s who were keen to blow this old-fashioned and static fashion style away, and to replace it with clothes that really did answer the needs of the younger women. These designers were young themselves, they were frequently women and they worked with talented young photographers, models, and fashion editors who also wanted to shake up fashion and banish the 'dressing like your mother' image for ever.

While some of these new young fashion designers did use floral print in the late 1950s and early 1960s, it was the exception rather than the rule. The energy of these designers and the modernity that they embodied meant that this was the lead that fashion would follow in the new decade. Did this mean that the floral frock was forgotten and would be left behind? Indeed, was there a future for the floral frock, or had it found its optimum style and would remain stagnated in the basic shirtwaister style for ever?

To find out how the floral frock survived into the 1960s with new styles and new treatments, you have to look at the customer who was a little older than the very young women to whom the younger London fashion designers were selling their clothes. It is women in their late 20s and early 30s, women who were thinking about new homes and young families, rather than about shopping for clothes on the King's Road in London, who ensured that the floral frock lived on in the early 1960s.

July 1959
Joyce wears a floral frock on a picnic with her aunt at Lytham St Annes, Lancashire. She made the dress, in white piqué cotton with small flowers in shades of maroon, especially for the visit to her relatives.
Private collection

OPPOSITE PAGE **1964**
Detail of a floral printed silk evening dress by Jean Muir for Jane and Jane with a design of small flowers, leaves and blackberries.
Fashion Museum

June 1961
Setting off on holiday to Broadstairs
from her home in North Cheam, Surrey,
Evelyn wears a yellow floral frock which
she made of fabric from John Lewis in
Oxford Street, London.
Private collection

In a way, perhaps these women chose the traditional floral frock because they did want to look like their mothers. It could be said that a shirtwaister floral frock would give them maturity, or help them to fulfill or to see themselves in their roles as wives and mothers. The floral frock meant that they had the right clothes for the job of being mothers themselves and looking after homes and young families. Wearing a floral frock that wasn't that dissimilar to a dress that your mother might wear meant that you were assuming the mantle of your mother. The daughter becomes the mother, and she indicates that in the clothes she chooses to wear.

There were also of course practical considerations in that floral frocks were easy to launder and to keep looking fresh and pretty, a consideration when dealing with twin tubs and babies and small children. A basic floral frock or a floral skirt was also relatively easy, cheap and quick to make. Floral skirts became more popular in the late 1950s and early 1960s, an instance of 'borrowing' a garment style from holiday wear and turning it into fashionable day wear. The move to wear more floral skirts and tops at this date can also be seen as an indicator of the increased casualisation of dress, and the first steps towards the fashion for separates, a trend which has become so important in later 20th century fashion.

June 1961
Both the floral skirt and the floral frock, worn here for a visit to relatives, were made by the wearers. The fabric for the skirt was bought on a market stall, while the dress fabric is not unlike the design on the left with leaves and petals blending into one another.
Private collection
Fashion Museum

85

It's true to say that floral frocks in the early 1960s became much brighter with the flowers in the textile designs drawn in strong toning or contrasting colours. The ground colour of the textile prints were sometimes different colours, rather than the standard white ground of the 1950s, or the darker colours of the 1920s and 1930s. There was often too a busy-ness and exuberance in the textile design with simple almost stylised flower shapes rendered in bold colours and a bold hand, a marked contrast to the careful drawing often seen in the textile designs of the floral frocks of the 1950s.

October 1961
Flo and Mabel wear floral frocks and pearls during a visit to their brother to attend their niece's wedding.
Private collection

Early 1960s
Two American floral frocks in bright colours and assured floral designs. The dress on the left is made of silk and is by the fashion store Lord and Taylor. The dress on the right is cotton sateen. Although one is sleeveless and the other has short sleeves, both floral frocks have the smooth bodice without a collar typical of early 1960s dresses.
Fashion Museum

Early 1960s
Guests at a wedding in Surrey chose
floral frocks in a variety of styles.
Private collection

Floral frocks in the early 1960s did follow the line established in the 1950s with a tight belted waist and a flaring skirt. But there was a new shape in the Paris and London couture and from the ready-to-wear fashion houses, as well as from the new, young fashion designers. A slender shaped dress, which would eventually become the shift, and then the mini-dress, became fashionable at this time and examples can be seen incorporating the use of floral print.

It was perhaps this new shape for dresses which marked the beginning of the end of the golden age of the floral frock. Somehow the tighter more linear shape did not lend itself to the exuberant use of floral print, with bold colours, intricate drawings and big repeats. This kind of textile design needed big skirts to work to its full effect. While the flaring skirt style was kept alive for a time at the beginning of the 1960s, fashion moved on to a different shape. A new type of textile design would be needed if floral print was going to continue to be part of fashionable dress.

Early 1960s
Pink flowers in an all-over pattern on a silk floral frock with a large bow at the waist by Jane Andre of California.
Fashion Museum

OPPOSITE PAGE **July 1963**
Rosa in a floral two-piece in a field near Skipton, North Yorkshire.
Private collection

Fashion always finds something new, and new ways of dealing with floral print were developed in the 1960s. But what is interesting to note is that although the golden age of the floral frock as a fashionable garment was drawing to a close in the mid-1960s, women continued to wear floral frocks in the styles from the 1950s, and earlier. This is particularly marked in women of older years, who continued to be true to the styles of their youth.

The legacy of the golden age of the floral frock continues to this day, not only in our memories and as a means to visualise, imagine or construct the past, but also in dresses incorporating floral print. Today, if you look on the streets of any town or village in Britain on a summer day women of a certain age, women who were young in the 1950s and 1960s, are still wearing floral frocks. But floral print isn't confined to the older generation. Younger women are discovering the joys of floral print; that it can be pretty and feminine, and can help to make you feel happy and attractive on a sunny day. With recent fashions in wrap dresses – with sinuous, naturalistic or geometric floral print – and floral print tunics or tops, worn over jeans, the floral frock, an unlikely fashion hero of the mid-20th century, lives on today.

June 1965
A floral frock for a visit to see the grandchildren.
Private collection

Part two

Floral frocks for the modern age

The 1960s

By 1963 the media had become obsessed with youth and newness, and by the mid-1960s youth had the biggest impact on art, design and popular culture. Cultural historians and commentators have retrospectively acknowledged that before 1945 youth culture had not existed, and by the 1960s children born directly after the war had become a social and consumer group in their own right, i.e. by 1964 8% (4 million) of the British population were aged 15-19.[1] The juxtaposition of both social and consumer group is not incidental; young people had started to forge a group mentality and identity through consumer choices (i.e. clothing, music, cinema, and popular culture in general), although often these were contradictory, embracing both a rejection of middle-class bourgeois ideology and the emergent affluence associated with a post-war consumer culture. This meant that new markets for clothing were being formed, but these were largely based on the development of a new and affluent youth consumer group.

The significance of youth was not merely a response to emergent numbers of young people. Consistent low inflation and virtual full employment created a buoyant economy sustained by greater disposable income, increased access to credit and consumer goods. In terms of a collective consciousness, youth culture in the 1960s emerged from a cross-cultural response to Americana and the genre of the 'Angry Young Man', brought to life in aggressive acts of rebellion, resulting from class distinction and social dissatisfaction throughout the early post-war

PAGES 94/95 **Mid-1960s**
Detail of a floral printed silk twill shift dress by J. Tiktiner with design of several giant pink flowers and scrolling leaves.
Fashion Museum

OPPOSITE PAGE **1960s**
Detail of a floral printed cotton shift dress by Linda Leigh with design of loosely drawn roses and leaves.
Private collection

1   Nigel Whiteley, *Pop Design: From Modernism to Mod*, Thames & Hudson, London, p.15

decades. Although violent behaviour was largely associated with members of subcultures and to isolated incidents, rebellion became synonymous with youth.

Youthful rebellion was not limited to anti-social behaviour; it was endemic throughout culture, represented in the rejection of the ideology of earlier generations and in new patterns of consumption and display. An emphasis on 'youth' as a group, concept and consciousness, highlighted and privileged the 'new', a consequence of which was a focus on the 'here and now' rather than a projected vision of the future. The easier availability of credit offered consumers potential access to goods otherwise outside their financial reach, as well as instant gratification. Valorisation centred on the novel, the fashionable, and therefore systematically fostered a culture of obsolescence, in which longevity was negated.

Obsolescence became a standard within product design, with goods having a limited 'life-span'. Similarly, new, disposable materials became an innovative expression of the element of society defined as ultimately modern (living solely in the present). Furniture, a product group with traditionally a lengthy life-span, for example, was transformed by the introduction of cardboard or inflatable tables and chairs. Similarly, products emanating from disciplines which by design were ephemeral, such as fashion, became increasingly obsolescent with the development of paper and edible clothing.

One might presume that, with an emphasis on 'newness', motifs were revolutionised as a response to the immediacy of culture; this didn't really happen, although new motifs and forms of representation were added to 'traditional' forms and patterns like florals. To remove all remnants of the past would be to isolate design from its context and heritage, and how can one express 'newness' if there is no marker of the 'old'? We might see this then as a period of change and challenges, in terms of society and culture, but also in relation to forms of representation, constantly challenging existing boundaries in relation to shape, form, colour and style, and redressing them with remarkable regularity.

The return to past styles in order to effect their transformation, can be demonstrated in the revivalist tendencies exhibited by the renewed interest and popularity of the flea market,[2] second-hand shopping and mix-and-match.[3] The creation of a sense of individuality (in relation to interiors and fashion) from a variety of disparate sources, both old and new, was intended to highlight the eclectic, spontaneous and throw-away mood of the times. The past or the 'old' was resurrected through re-appropriation, used as a dressing-up box of visual signs and references that could enhance or comment on the contemporary world.[4]

The new attitudes to the past, were tinged with both Romanticism and nostalgia. In an age defined by a cult of the new, the past took on a new meaning: one of loss, without being 'lost'. The effect of such an analogy manifested itself in a variety of ways in

OPPOSITE PAGE **June 1964**
A long-sleeved floral frock with matching headscarf by Hilary Hucknell for Liberty in this photograph for *Vogue* fashion magazine. The day of the New Look inspired or shirtwaister floral frock was passing to be replaced by new more rectangular shaped dresses. If floral frocks were to survive then new ways of arranging floral motifs on fabric needed to be developed. Strong linear design, such as this, was one way forward.
Peter Rand/Vogue © The Condé Nast Publications Ltd

2   Raphael Samuel, *Theatres of Memory*, Verso, 1994
3   Mary Quant, *Quant by Quant*, Cassell and Co Ltd, 1966; see also Nigel Whiteley, op. cit., pp.20-25
4   Marni Fogg, *Boutique*, Mitchell Beazley, 2003, pp. 155-163

relation to design; the styles of past eras were revived, i.e. Art Nouveau,[5] as well as garments indicative of changing attitudes to gender and sexuality (a symptom of the permissive society) and notions of the creative spirit, such as a reappraisal of 19th century Romanticism in menswear. Effectively, though, these attempts at revivalism were purely aesthetic; the original intent of the designs, motifs and garments were merely a stylistic nod to the past, rather than an attempt to embrace original ideologies and meaning. The past became a reference, a reaction, an expression of style rather than design with substance, paying lip-service to continuity in a time of contradiction and change.

The period is frequently understood as revolutionary, embracing and witnessing transformations in relation to gender, racial and sexual politics. These 'revolutionary' tendencies, combined with the new found cult of youth, influenced fashion and design, i.e. the Lolita look, which exploited a child-like youthfulness mixed with a sexual knowingness, embodied by the models Twiggy and Jean Shrimpton, and demonstrated in the fashion for baby-doll dresses, ditsy floral prints and childish motifs. This ambiguous approach to youth suggests innocence corrupted; the transition from child to woman.

New forms of communication such as television facilitated the circulation of fashionable styles and trends. Programmes aimed directly at a youth audience such as *Ready, Steady, Go!* promoted new designs, designers and styles and created new

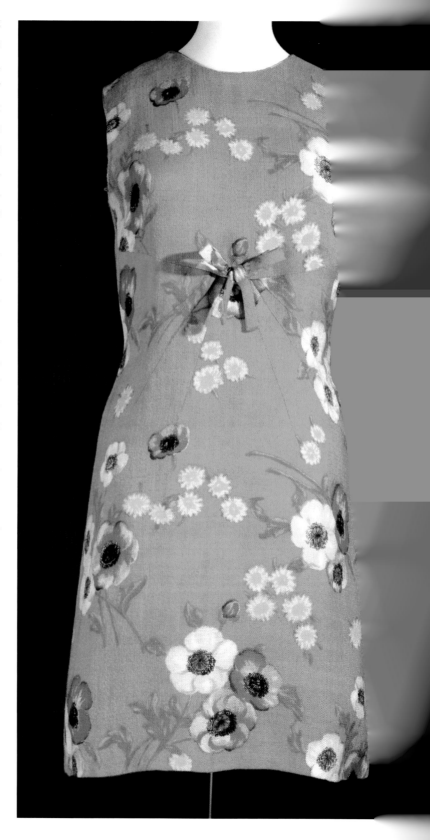

5   Barbara Hulanicki, *From A to Biba*, Hutchinson, 1983

fashionable icons. The role of the media, along with new means of buying clothing, questioned the dominance of couture, consigning it to the past, a revolution which was to have a profound effect on the fashion industry to the present day.

By the late 1960s, youth culture itself had transformed, embracing not just the mood of the times but political and social events. Most notably this manifested itself in 'flower power', the hippy movement, and a general awareness of ethical and environmental concerns. The changing emphasis of youth culture from one based on newness, consumerism and membership of youth groups towards one based on a collective consciousness was seemingly far more revolutionary than preceding youth movements. Here the ideological perspective was a focus on redressing the status quo, becoming more attuned to global issues and the effects of mass consumerism, which enabled fashion to develop and to draw influence from a new set of cultural referents. In particular, the influence of the East, in terms of print techniques (batik, tie-dye and block printing) and motifs, such as exotic flora and fauna, bright colours and so on, became a sign of anti-establishmentism and of global harmony. Similarly, the effects of hallucinogenic drugs and a move towards psychedelic design motifs, patterns and colours encouraged the surreal expression of print in fashion. Free-flowing forms replaced hard-edged geometrics and ordered floral designs, suggested nature, like youth, 'gone wild'.

Mid-1960s
A new format for the floral frock: bold and bright coloured shift dresses. The bright blue synthetic linen dress with flashes of colours in the red poppies and yellow flowers is by The White House; the white silk dress with large pink exotic flowers is by J. Tiktiner.
Fashion Museum

The most significant expression of the fusion of textile design with fashion was demonstrated in the collaboration between Ossie Clark and Celia Birtwell. Clark's sinuous designs addressed feminine shape with masculine tailoring,[6] whilst Birtwell's mix of bold floral motifs and abstract lines challenged the relationship between and possibilities of fashion and textiles in an unprecedented way.

Classified as an era marked by a cultural revolution, the 1960s heralded the beginning of new attitudes to fashionable dress. With a focus on youth and newness, followed by an emphasis on Green politics, the period witnessed a redress and questioning of exactly what it was to be 'fashionable'. It was a period, in terms of design, which challenged boundaries between high and low culture, old and new, mix and match and cultural fusion. For floral design this was an era of change and challenge; from small and ditsy girly prints through to the over-sized designs associated with flower power, patterns swung between the sublime and the ridiculous.

6   Marnie Fogg, op. cit., p.163

May 1964
A head to toe floral look with the
same print used on a matching long-
sleeved dress and pair of stockings.
Fashion Museum

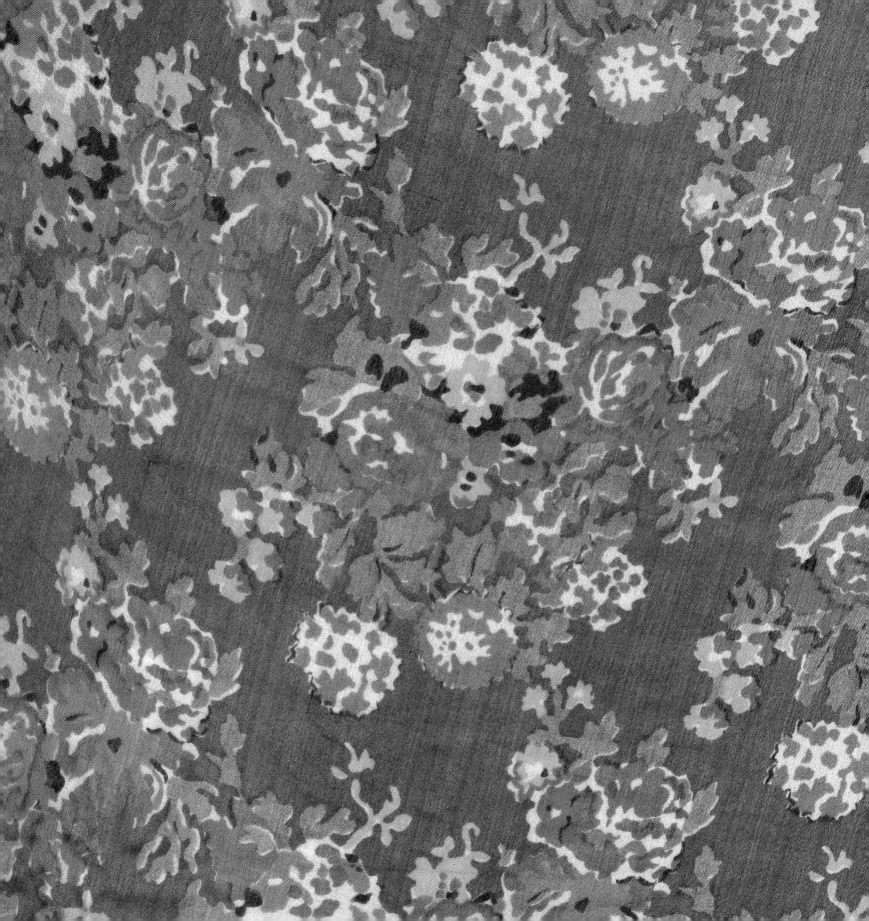

The 1970s

By the 1970s, fashion was in flux. The dominance of couture had been challenged as a result of the impact of youth culture and post-war restoration, and the associated rise of consumerism emerging as a response to post-war affluence offered access to fashionable goods to a much wider proportion of the population. This meant that the general population had greater access to fashion magazines, the fashionable media (including television) and fashionable clothing available in new high street stores. Fashion was diffusing and being re-appropriated much more quickly, and notions of what it was to be fashionable became more vague. In essence, the notion of fashion had become less stable, and consequently new styles, fabrics and fashion icons emerged from a variety of different sources, from couture to popular culture, from peer groups and beyond.

It wasn't just fashion that was undergoing a transformation: the 1970s encapsulates a period of social and cultural confusion, of war and rebellion, economic decline (inflation was 27% in 1975) and environmentalism, which fused the local with the global in unprecedented ways. The threat of potential social disarray exemplified by Watergate and the impeachment of a US president, the rise of trade unionism ('the winter of discontent' in the early 1970s) and impending strikes and accompanying shortages, and an increasing concern about world energy resources challenged the status quo as never before.[7] The future didn't look great, as the promise of post-war restoration failed to materialise to any

OPPOSITE PAGE **Mid-1970s**
Detail of a long sleeved floral printed silk day dress by John Bates.
Fashion Museum

7   Christopher Booker, *The Seventies: Portrait of a Decade*, London, Allen Lane, 1980, p.4

great extent. Reaction or resistance to such social instability and its potential for chaos at this time can be demonstrated by turning towards that which offers stability. This manifested itself in increased worldwide conservatism, and by a fearful nostalgia for the past.

In relation to fashion, an underlying fear for the future and socio-cultural disillusion was expressed by, as Booker notes:

> 'Two unfailing barometers of cultural optimism in our century have been the height of buildings and the height of girls' hem-lines. In times of high excitement, like the Twenties and the Sixties, when people looked forward to the future with hope, the skyscrapers and the skirts went up. At times when men became fearful of the future, or began to look back nostalgically to the past, as in the early Thirties and the Seventies, they stopped building towers and the skirts came down again… Never, in either case, was the reaction so complete as it had been in the Seventies.'[8]

The decade it seems is best represented as the antithesis of the 1960s, rather than a continuation of it. None the less, no decade exists in isolation, and the seeds of change that caused so much worry in the 1970s[9] were sown decades earlier. Equally, the consequences of the rebellion of the 1960s were being felt for many years later, much of which can be viewed positively. For example, the impact of second wave feminism had far-reaching effects which politically were only starting to be realised in the 1970s. In Britain, the Equal Opportunities Act (1976) emerged after a long struggle between workers and employers, and feminism no longer seemed to speak from the margins as it became normalised within society.

The impact of feminism was not purely political; it impacted on women's lives and questioned the construction of femininity. By the mid-1970s notions of what women's roles were in society were becoming more diverse and inclusive. Women's magazines of the period started to mix political activism ('Action Woman' in *Woman* for example) with more traditional pursuits such as knitting and sewing patterns, and female role models included 'superwomen'[10] such as the round-the-world yachtswoman, Claire Francis, and the future Prime Minister, Margaret Thatcher. Fashion was still a large feature of these magazines, but the emphasis moved significantly from high fashion and difficult to wear garments to more practical and washable clothing. Similarly, dressmaking and knitting patterns focused on ease of making, projects that could be constructed in a matter of hours, emphasising a shift in the notion of 'women's work'.

Femininity appeared to be in crisis; women became increasingly unsure of what their social role was, and how they should look. The wearing of make-up, for example, instilled guilt in women who were sympathetic to the ideals of feminism, whilst others were suspicious of stepping outside the remits of fashion and into dungarees. Such a conflict seems to have impacted on the fashion industry to the extent that womenswear design

8 Ibid., p.6.
9 Ibid., p.7
10 This term was popularised by Shirley Conran through her book of the same name published in 1978

OPPOSITE PAGE **May 1972**
A halter necked floral printed sundress with a shirred bodice by Pablo and Delia, accessorised with a far from understated floral headdress.
Barry Lategan/Vogue © The Condé Nast Publications Ltd

was marked by, to a certain extent, a monotony and a frivolity or decadence. One might consider this to be the perfect expression of contemporary femininity, with such a juxtaposition indicative of confusion without an easy solution.

The destabilising of the constituents of femininity and the introduction of what can be described as a 'new woman' was an ideology embraced by and communicated to women through the media and educational institutions. Women had the potential to compete on a seemingly level playing field and, although women had always worked, the emphasis of new femininity was to work to fulfil one's goals and potential. Women, though, still had families, and this transition was not easy. Although there were new opportunities, the old roles still existed, and new career choices became merged with looking glamorous, keeping a successful home and family, and presenting oneself as the perfect hostess whilst entertaining.

This was an era of home entertaining. Dinner parties held at home rather than in restaurants became de rigueur, and although the art of cooking for such an occasion was demystified with recipes in women's magazines, dressing for dinner was still largely formal for women. The popularity of new man-made fabrics such as Crimplene, Qiana, Enkacrepe and Tricelon, and blended fibres such as Viyella and Trevira 2000, which were easy to print on and took colour well, enabled women of all ages and incomes to participate in the glamour of evening entertaining.

The new fabrics encouraged experimentation with print and pattern, and design motifs became bolder as a result. Similarly, the popularity of full-length dresses provided a larger canvas on which to experiment, and the luxury of exotic prints became mainstream.

The new trend towards boldness in pattern design was not merely a response to changing attitudes to femininity or to technological advancement; it was representative of a Zeitgeist that embraced domesticity (including the female form) as tactile, sensual and sexual. Perhaps this was a response to the ageing of a permissive generation, but the 1970s saw interior design and the beautifying of the home as increasingly tactile and potentially erotic. Adverts for products as disparate as carpets and china promoted luxury and excess as an extension of the body, and consequently the domestic took on almost fetishistic qualities. Ultimately such advertising stimulated desire in a new way; this was less about 'keeping up with the Joneses' and more about lust-induced longing. Consumer goods became associated firmly with desire, and their promotion as 'lifestyle' objects fuelled a desire which gave the consumer/owner/wearer access to a world of fantasy, a means of escaping the harsh realities of daily life. As Elizabeth Cowie acknowledged:

'Fantasy itself is characterised not by the achievement of wished-for objects but by the arranging of, a setting out of, the desire for certain objects'.[11]

OPPOSITE PAGE **December 1971**
A modern take on the historic use of floral print as a panel or part of a dress. Bill Gibb designed this dress for Twiggy to wear to the premiere of the film *The Boyfriend* in Los Angeles. *Fashion Museum*

11 Elizabeth Cowie, 'Pornography and Fantasy Psychoanalytic Perspectives', in L Segal & M McIntosh (eds) *Sex Exposed: Sexuality and the Pornography Debate*, London: Virago, 1992, p.136, quoted in *Rebecca Arnold, Fashion Desire and Anxiety*, London: I B Tauris, 2001, p. 71.

So, consumer goods became, by association, fantasy 'lifestyle' choices, stimulating desire, not just for the goods themselves, but for access to a world of fantasy. Essentially, the consumer was seduced by the promise offered by consumer goods. Fantasy in the 1970s was linked inexorably with sex and sensuality, and although this wasn't a new idea as fashion had always been seen as 'extraordinary' rather than ordinary, and associated with sex and the body, it manifested itself far more explicitly. Both prints and dresses embraced this new and brazen fusion of sex and fashion by focusing on two areas; firstly fusing the exotic with the erotic, and secondly by emphasising the potential for clothing to both reveal and conceal the body.

Boundaries were being broken down, as were accepted fashion norms, so to see floral motifs combining with revealing and overtly sexual dress designs was no longer unusual. The innocence of the floral motif had been corrupted. Fashion and glamour were now decadent and debauched, offering a stark contrast to the social and economic climate of the time.

Exotic floral motifs mixed with loose, long-length and flowing garments became synonymous with a hedonistic and debauched narcissism emanating from fashion at the time. Reference to the exotic had historically been symbolically linked to the erotic, of 'otherness' and of distant places and cultures. By the 1970s this association spoke through hot-house flowers and colour, bold print and re-appropriation of designs from India, China and Japan. The emphasis of cultural fusion in the creation of 'erotic' designs bore testimony to the heritage of Art Nouveau, drawing emotive rather than stylistic inspiration from the work of artists and designers such as Aubrey Beardsley. Designs expressed heat, and by association the loosening of clothes as well as morality.

The fluidity of garments emphasised the body, through sinuous lines and simple cuts, by both revealing and concealing simultaneously. All clothing has the potential to reveal and conceal the body, but the fluidity of the longer dressses of the 1970s appears to do both at the same time. Covering the body in a fabric which falls and moves in accordance with the wearer is seductive as it acts as a mirror to the body. The garment, in motion, outlines the contours of the body hinting, as in strip-tease, at what lies beneath.

Many of these garments by designers such as Bellville Sassoon, Bill Gibb, John Bates and Jeff Banks were featured on the pages of *Vogue*, and were worn by more wealthy and Bohemian members of society. These influenced high street styles by Laura Ashley. Liberty prints and floral fabrics were available at department stores such as John Lewis which enabled the home dressmaker to recreate designs at a fraction of the cost.

Such a state of social and cultural confusion led, as one might expect, to an eclecticism of styles, shapes and motifs in fashion, but one enduring design theme of the period encompasses and reflects this instability; heritage and tradition.

Like the motifs and styles favoured by the Romantic Aesthetes of the 19th century, floral motifs also, and conversely, adopted a quality which emphasised a tragic beauty; of innocence lost. Prints were also muted and soft, faded, reminiscent of the passing of time, age weary and worn. This was an explicit nostalgia which seemed to open the doors of a historic wardrobe, taking inspiration from the dust covered and sun damaged contents.

The most significant design company exhibiting this theme was Liberty, which in 1975 celebrated its centenary. Founded by Arthur Liberty in 1875, the company's roots were firmly embedded in an Art Nouveau mentality and the centenary collections reflected this heritage. In particular the 1920s 100% cotton fabric 'Tana Lawn', named after the Lake Tana region in Sudan where the raw cotton grew, and 'Lawn' from the fine weave from which the fabric was constructed, regained popularity (although it is possible to say that it never went out of style). Tana lawn became firmly associated in the popular psyche with ditsy floral prints synonymous with a 'Liberty' style.

Liberty style, because of its seeming timelessness, maintained its popularity as a result of its widespread appeal. This appeal can be assessed as the expression of three key themes that have been maintained throughout the history of Liberty's. These include the use of high quality fabrics, use of floral print and the ability to move with the times and adapt fabric design accordingly.

1970s
A floral printed cotton day or evening dress by Laura Ashley. The dress mixes two different floral pattern: one design is of naturalistic flowers in a western tradition; the second more stylised and geometric print owes more to a Middle Eastern or Indian aesthetic.
Fashion Museum

The use of high quality fabrics will always make a product desirable.[12] Similarly, the ability to adapt to suit the mood of the times rather than embracing the avant-garde of high fashion has enabled Liberty prints and garments to transcend the innovativeness and un-wearablity of 'new' fashion styles. This created a sense of the 'timeless', heightening longevity and widening market appeal. This approach is almost an anti-fashion statement, with prints and garments appealing to and associated with wealthy old ladies and trendy young things alike. Generational distances were bridged by Liberty and as a consequence the designs appeared organic – as if they grew there – seemingly having always existed.[13]

This longevity and continued popularity was also a response to an understanding of floral motifs in popular culture. Seen as 'natural' and inherently 'beautiful', floral motifs are understood as inoffensive – one can't be offended by nature in the same way as one might be by abstraction, for example. The inoffensiveness emanating from an understanding of floral motifs and patterns in design also suggests that they are not challenging, and that they therefore exist outside the dynamic world of fashion. Motifs, styles and technology all contribute to the changing representation of florals. Patterns, colours and techniques used in floral frocks are widely varied, and yet the association of them with an unchanging timelessness seems hard to shake.

Themes of the organic and the timeless deriving from under-

1970s
Detail of a floral printed cotton day dress made by a home dressmaker from Liberty Tana lawn.
Fashion Museum

12   See Lou Taylor 'De-coding the Hierarchy of Fashion Textiles' in C Boydell & M Schoeser (eds), *Disentangling Textiles*, Middlesex University Press, 2002
13   Peter York, 'Style Wars', in John Thackara, *Design After Modernism*, Thames and Hudson, 1988

standings of floral motifs in design are linked to constructs of heritage and national identity. National identity is formulated from a series of ideological themes and compositions which loosely establish a collective sense of belonging. As it is virtually impossible to create a cohesive mentality for a population, themes and compositions arise and are sustained through rather general connections, such as values, language and iconography. Floral motifs are very much part of this; they relate particularly to the nation and the iconography of the landscape. Specifically in Britain, floral motifs relate not just to a sense of 'home', but also to the history of the nation, referring to times when Britain was 'Great'. So floral prints that correlate with 'Britishness' tend to refer back to the 19th century, to the Arts and Crafts Movement, to William Morris, to colonialism and to simpler times. This means that British national identity, particularly that which is expressed through a 'natural' aesthetic, articulates 'home' as 'homesick', and is a product of nostalgia, looking back to times that are lost.

Similarly, British style has an inherent link to the class system, and floral frocks speak of the leisure class and aristocracy. Hardy Amies noted that:

'The English woman usually has some feel of the country about her clothes. I think that until six o'clock she likes to look like a woman who has come up from the country for the day and does not live in London. That is a contrast to the French woman who likes to look as though she were born and bred in Paris and would be awfully bored to leave it'.[14]

Amies's assertion that women's style appeared to be linked with an association with the landed gentry is rather far fetched, but none the less may account for the continued popularity of floral prints in fashion design throughout the century.

Liberty prints were predominantly linked to this endemic sense of loss, class, of heritage, and a desire to recreate past times. Indeed, Liberty prints remain to this day so tied up with a British national identity that they have become travel souvenirs for UK visitors. In a similar vein, but on a smaller budget, Laura Ashley prints aimed to recreate a sense of a lost Britishness reminiscent of both a Colonial heritage[15] and what Alison Lurie calls the 'English Shepherdess costume'.[16] This was about dressing up, playing a part. As a fashion feature in June 1975 entitled 'This Summer's Flowering of a Million Hours' opened:

'Writing of almost a hundred years ago Isadora Duncan said: "I bought a few yards of veiling at Liberty in which I appeared at Mrs X's party". She danced for joy. Yves Saint Laurent, Salvador, Jean Muir, Bill Gibb and John Bates chose Liberty prints, new ones, and old archive prints refreshed with new colours from Susan Collier's Centenary and Special collections. They designed the dresses on these pages. And now you can dance.'[17]

The editorial seems to recognise a mood of loss combined with tragic beauty and by quoting the fated dancer, Isadora Duncan,

14 Hardy Amies, 'wool in fashion' lecture at the Royal Society of Arts, 1954. Published by the Department of the International Wool Secretariat, quoted in De La Haye A and Glenville T, 'Country', in De La Haye (ed), *The Cutting Edge: 50 Years of British Fashion*, London: V&A Publishing, 1996, p.125

15 See J Woodham, *Twentieth Century Design*, 1997, p.210, who notes that Colonial revivalism was popular in interior decoration at the time as well

16 A Lurie, *The Language of Clothes*, New York: Owl, 1981, p.104

17 'This Summer's Flowering of a Million Hours', *Vogue*, June, 1975

whose penchant for flowing fabrics was to be her downfall, emphasises the relationship of the present with the past.

By the late 1970s the mood had changed and the two strands of debauched glamour and nostalgia merged into a more pastoral and romantic theme, which embraced new interpretations of the floral dress. This style incorporated flounces, cinched-in waists and a mixture of pattern. Referred to throughout the period as the 'Romantic' or 'Gypsy' look, floral printed dresses encapsulated a new 'aspirational' and 'global' woman.

The 'Gypsy' look was easy to create and borrowed iconography from the rural peasant communities of Eastern Europe, although it really bore little relation to authentic Romany dress. Skirts were wide, tiered and flowing, whilst bodices were loose, and necklines off-the shoulder. The look was layered, which meant that old and new clothes could be combined, whilst patterns, techniques such as print or embroidery, and fabrics could also be mixed. Described as 'Second World Chic' by Alison Lurie,[18] the style demonstrated a global affinity, but also expressed a passion associated with these cultures.

Vogue anticipated this combination of new fashion and feminine ideals combined with lifestyle consumerism, when a fashion feature noted that the Romantic style spoke to a specific kind of woman:

'She'd like to teach the world to sing in perfect harmony. She's a believer in love at first sight, a tarot card reader, a collector of ghost stories, a confidante. She has lunch at San Lorenzo, dinner at Tramps, tea for two under the pergola. She'll only wear clothes with good vibrations – in other words, soft cool, free dresses, camisoles and cotton skirts. Her music: Vivaldi and Dylan... Her luggage: a carpet bag she picked up at a country auction, assorted straw baskets. Her transport: bus, Porsche, bicycle. Her natural habitat: home with faded prints, honeysuckle, herbs and French provincial furniture. Her holiday: a cottage in Wales, a farmhouse in Lucca, a schooner round the isles of Greece – but she doesn't have to travel to relax, her whole life's a holiday'.[19]

This new woman was a traveller, a free spirit – her own woman, decadent, fragrant and in tune with the environment. Her life, constructed from a variety of cultural references, fusing the past with the present, escaping into a bohemian fantasy. This is a rural idyll for the contemporary world; a world which mixes the traditional with the modern, for example, the bicycle with a sports car, a rural Welsh holiday with the glamour and excess of yachting around the Greek Islands. In this respect the 'simple life' can be understood as effortlessly transcending the mundane and the everyday. Similarly, like Lurie's assertion, the concept of a rural idyll only manifests itself in fashion when it displays the iconography and ideology of the countryside without evidence of rural toil.[20] The past is cleaned up and made palatable for a contemporary audience.

18 A Lurie, op. cit., pp.97-98
19 'Romantic' fashion feature, *Vogue*, June 1974

20 A Lurie, op. cit., p.104

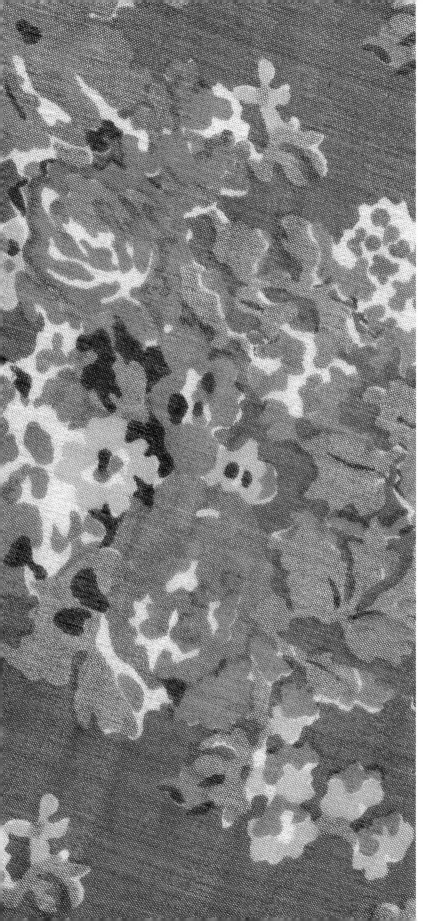

In reality, of course, few women had access to this type of life, but it did offer access to a lifestyle regardless of budget. For relatively low cost women could purchase a small part of this, baskets, Laura Ashley dresses or other ephemera associated with dressing up which were available in high street stores or in catalogues. In this way, a floral frock was symbolic of an escape from the realities of the modern world to live the dream of the truly 'modern' woman.

It is possible to suggest that the 1970s, as a period of turbulent social and global issues, created a climate of instability and fear. Fashion and textile design responded to these conditions by wallowing in a decadent and faded glamour associated with the past, or by attempting to recreate more stable times through a nostalgic longing.

Changing attitudes to femininity also encompassed this feeling of loss. Femininity was confused and resulted in a more overtly sexual approach to the female form, either through notions of revealing and concealing, or through lifestyle and consumer choices which demonstrated a more empowered woman, in control of her environment and life in general. Similarly, whilst feminism promoted an anti-fashion approach to dress, fashion itself adopted an anti-'fashion' stance by returning to feminine motifs of the past.

Mid-1970s
Detail of a long sleeved floral printed
silk day dress by John Bates.
Fashion Museum

The 1980s

The 1980s is often characterised as a period of excess, of yuppies, money and greed, personified by the character Gordon Gekko in the film *Wall Street*. However, although this image may well have been the case for an urban minority, the majority of the population did not share in this new affluence. Like the 1930s, Britain was divided into areas of boom and slump, with the prosperous South diametrically opposed to de-industrialisation in the North. The period was dominated by Thatcherism, moves towards design and enterprise, the miners' strike, globalisation and the domination of multi-national corporations, race riots, concerns regarding the spread of HIV and AIDS, war in the Falklands, excess and poverty, with the vast media coverage of famine in Ethiopia and Sudan.

The period also witnessed the end of the Cold War, increased conservatism in global politics with little left-wing dissension, and a move towards the cult of the individual. The culmination of these historical, political, economic, social and cultural conditions which matured in the 1980s were indicative of a climate of post-modernity. In terms of visual culture, post-modernism manifests itself in a variety of ways, all of which rely on a critical and questioning approach to accepted norms. Initially, post-modernism questions, and often fuses, hierarchical boundaries and classifications, that is culture and society, high and low culture, past and future, and space and time. As such, post-modernism encourages bricolage (the collecting and collaging of

OPPOSITE PAGE **Early 1980s**
Detail of a floral printed cotton
ensemble by Wendy Dagworthy.
Fashion Museum

images, references and ideas), often in an ironic manner, to make a new statement. So, motifs and styles from different historical eras co-exist with seemingly clashing patterns and materials, soft objects appear hard, feminine references mix with the masculine, and so on and vice versa.

The 'anything goes' mentality that seems to permeate post-modernism is largely the result of what has been described as the dissolution of 'grand' or 'meta' narratives. A 'meta' narrative is an ultimate truth, something, usually a system of belief, which is fixed. By the late 1960s these were increasingly called into question; so, the dominance of organised Religion, the Monarchy, the law, history, and so on, were seen as unstable, no longer beyond question or inherently 'truthful', creating a sense of confusion. Life was becoming increasingly fragmented, partially as a result of the mass media and an increased circulation of images, signs and messages. If nothing could be classified as 'true' or indeed 'real', then by definition everything could be, and the individual had the potential to create a sense of 'reality' by piecing together fragments of the multiplicity of 'realities' circulating.

By the 1980s, post-modernism became a major influence in design and fashion. The dominance of couture, which had been destabilised in the 1960s, became far more evident, with street styles and fabrics inspiring catwalk collections. Examples include denim, dungarees, day-glow and graffiti motifs, which highlighted a 'bubble up' trajectory in fashion trends and also dem-

onstrated a fusion of high and low culture. Similarly, patterns and styles drew reference from the past, the present and the future, mixing and juxtaposing references and symbols from a variety of disparate sources, creating a sense of time/space confusion. Examples include the rich floral brocades and chintzes more usually associated with home furnishings, designed by Ralph Lauren and Kenzo (to name but two) that dominated the mid-to-late-1980s evening wear, or the wearing of ball gowns during the daytime, which was a fashion really only adopted by pop and media celebrities.

Indeed, fashion became an aspect of bricolage, a dressing-up box full of cultural and identity based references, a language which was understood universally.[21] Historical eras, cultures and specific garments were reduced to signs, representative of words, themes or moods. So mini skirts spoke of 'swinging London', of youth and newness, and history became a source of style inspiration waiting to be pillaged. In 1988, Christian Lacroix noted in *Vogue* that:

> *'Every one of my dresses possess a detail that can be connected with something historic, something from a past culture. We don't invent anything'.*[22]

Lacroix's acknowledgement that the inspiration for his collections in the 1980s came from the past questions the notion of fashion as dynamic and avant garde. As the battle-cry of Punks several years earlier of 'no future' bore testimony, the future of

OPPOSITE PAGE **April 1988**
Exaggerated sleeves, a plunging neckline and a short tight skirt in this bold floral printed two piece by Ungaro. *Arthur Elgort/Vogue © The Condé Nast Publications Ltd*

21 I Chambers, Popular Culture: *The Metropolitan Experience*, London: 1986, p.185
22 Claire Wilcox & Valerie Mendes, *Modern Fashion in Detail*, V&A Publishing, 1991, p.90, quoted in Christopher Breward, *The Culture of Fashion*, Manchester University Press, 1995, p.232

fashion lay in the past. Of course, the past was not wholly recreated, merely referenced and adapted to suit new consumers and markets. Often following a post-modern fragmentary rather than linear approach to history, styles from different historical periods were mixed and merged to create a 'new' look. This diverse appreciation of history was merely a surface or aesthetic response and lacked the depth and meaning of the original styles, garments and motifs. This was a period of style rather than substance and this eclectic fusion of ideas demonstrated a pastiche, a rather tongue-in-cheek and ironic nod to the past. Although it was unusual to see the historic costume inspired ensembles of the New Romantics outside major urban centres like London and Birmingham, it was normal to see ditsy, drop-waisted, over-sized[23] Laura Ashley dresses, mixed with floppy hats, footless or striped tights and Dr Martens shoes or boots. Likewise, second-hand dresses, over-sized men's jackets and military insignia were mixed with high street trends, creating an eclectic and somewhat personal response to fashion.

The fondness for what Angela McRobbie calls 'retro dressing'[24] demonstrated a desire to recreate the past in the present; not exactly or with any air of authenticity, but to create an essence of what had gone before. She noted that the popularity of second-hand clothing and vintage dresses had been superseded and exploited by the high street who were now offering new and mass manufactured 'vintage inspired' garments:

'...there is the so called 'tea dress', heavily advertised in the summers of both 1987 and 1988 by Laura Ashley, Next, Miss Selfridge and Warehouse. These are new visions of the high-quality 1930s and 1940s printed crepes sought out by girls and young women for many years, for the fall of their skirts and for their particularly feminine cut.'[25]

Bricolage was also used as an expression of globalisation, of cultural fusion and of political protest. Designers such as Wendy Dagworthy created outfits which were also a capsule wardrobe; a series of garments that could be mixed and matched or all worn together as a layered ensemble. Dagworthy's collections also had an ethical and ethnic component, referencing traditional costumes of eastern cultures, constructed from 'environmentally friendly' cotton.[26] This could be described as a global 'traveller' look, as layering and inter-changeability precluded the need for luggage. Further examples of this look could be seen in the collections of Kenzo, whose hothouse flower prints and vibrant colour-ways mixed with layered references taken from eastern and western cultures. The global traveller look filtered to the high street with the 1985 Laura Ashley collection marketed as:

'Summer Holiday clothes from Laura Ashley. Large floral prints in vibrant tropical colours of Peony and Khaki take their inspiration from the Polynesian Islands...'[27]

23 See Lee Wright, 'Outgrown Clothes for Grown-up People', in Juliet Ash and Elizabeth Wilson (eds), *Chic Thrills*, pp.49-57, for a discussion of the vogue for over-sized and under-sized clothing in the 1980s. This trend became the trademark for other new design companies such as BodyMap, which created garments which challenged the boundaries of gender and the body.

24 Angela McRobbie, 'Second Hand Dresses and the Role of the Ragmarket', in A McRobbie, *Postmodernism and Popular Culture*, Routlege, 1994, p148

25 Angela McRobbie, op.cit., p.139

26 See Christopher Breward et al, *The London Look*, p.144

27 Advert for Laura Ashley, *Vogue*, May, 1985

OPPOSITE PAGE **1980s**
Detail of an embroidered and appliqué cotton skirt by Wendy Dagworthy with a border of floral printed cotton. *Fashion Museum*

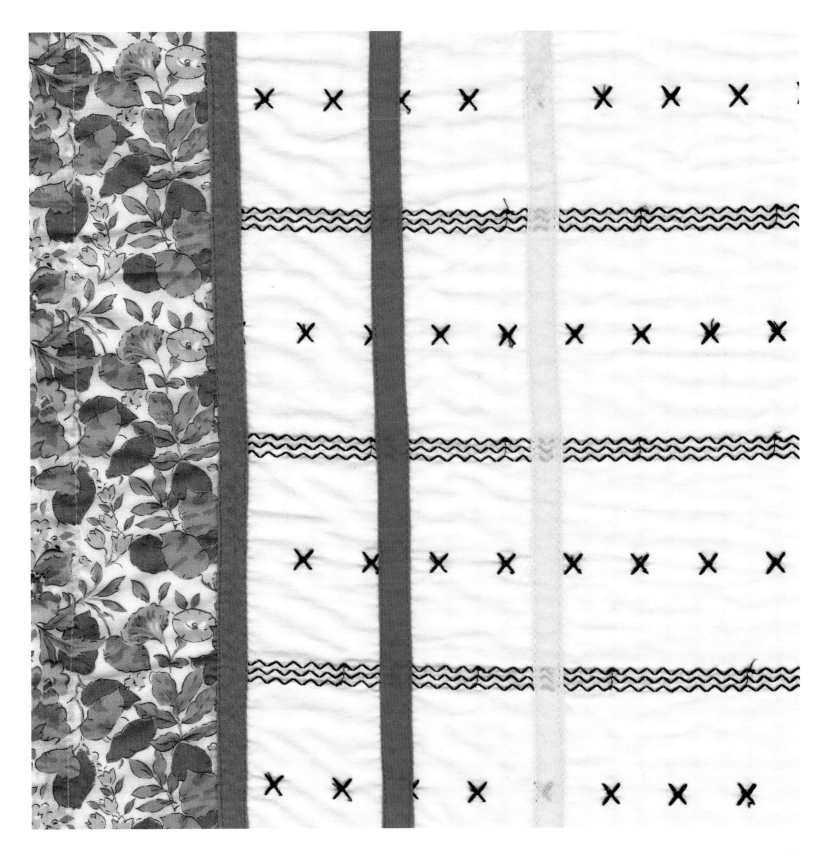

Over-sizing and shrink fitting, a fashion trend at the time, can also be seen as an expression of postmodernism (challenging the accepted boundaries and sizes of garments), as well as part of a layered bricolage. Over-sizing made a statement, either making the wearer appear more frail as in the layered look, or larger than life, as with power-dressing. We can therefore assume, that the sizing of garments expressed new modes of femininity – the assertive 'Superwoman' or the romantic waif. Women were presented as competing with men in the workplace and as a consequence fashion took influence from traditional menswear, creating tailored suits with padded shoulders to enhance the wearer's physical stature. Femininity was still in evidence, as frequently, hard-edged formal jackets were teamed with softer, more feminine blouses or accessories. Broad, padded shoulders were also evident in formal and informal dresses, blouses, jackets and coats.

The notion of bricolage as a facet of post-modernism was not merely the nostalgic yearnings of a confused society. Nor can it be seen as the expression of a quest for individuality as the 'looks' were as contrived and stylised as any couture collection of previous decades. However, the decade embraced the mass media and celebrity in unprecedented ways, and traditional role models and style icons were usurped by new fashion idols.

After the rebellion of the 1960s and 1970s and the rejection of traditional high culture, the style icon of the 1980s was remarkably a product of the social elite. From the announcement of her engagement to the Prince of Wales and subsequent marriage in 1981, through to her death in 1997, Lady Diana Spencer became the most photographed woman in the world, and an unlikely fashion icon. From her initial foray into the media limelight, the future Princess Diana was photographed wearing a New Edwardian look favoured by a group of wealthy and aristocratic young women, whom Peter York called 'Sloane Rangers'.[28] This look, including shirts with pie-crust collars, penny loafers, pearls and country styles for the City, disseminated very quickly on to the high street.[29]

Princess Diana's style evolved with her status; her initial awkwardness was replaced with the look of an independent woman, wearing collections from Bellville Sassoon and Versace, which not only enabled her to display modernity, but also a universal sex appeal.[30] Her clothes seemed to reflect the work or emotions she wanted to present at any given time; a good use for forwarding one's ideals and roles through fashion. Of course, clothing as a form of communication was hardly a new idea, but as it was expected that Princess Diana would be photographed, this was a means of communicating visually her good works. So when she gave speeches, she wore suits, when she wanted to present herself as a siren, she wore sequins, and when she wanted to appear as 'one of the people' or in a caring role, she wore floral patterns. This very basic semiotic approach to clothing and

28 Ann Barr and Peter York, *The Official Sloane Ranger's Handbook*, Angus Robertson Publishers, 1983

29 Angela McRobbie refers to the work of Angela Carter who had made studies of young women in the 1980s. She discovered that Princess Diana was a fashion and role model for young working class women, highlighting a class aspiration demonstrated through clothing choices. A McRobbie, op.cit., p.138.

30 T Graham & T Blanchard, *Dressing Diana*, Phoenix Illustrated, 1998, p.10

identity exploited the language of clothes, assuming that everyone would be able to read them.

Floral printed dresses in the 1980s embraced fashion as a form of visual communication by playing with signs and codes of dress, often in an ironic way. High and low cultural references merged, cultures fused, shapes changed, and the world of design saw history as a dressing-up box. Postmodernism created a climate of superficiality; nostalgic referents and the emulation of a social elite, power dressing and global travelling seemed to conceal the wide social cultural divide between rich and poor, and black and white.

Early 1980s
Detail of a floral printed cotton
ensemble by Wendy Dagworthy.
Fashion Museum

The 1990s

The 1990s can be seen retrospectively as a period of newness; a more mature, knowing era than that of the 1960s, but certainly one which looked to the past and to the future simultaneously, in a tentatively optimistic way. This was an era of regeneration; of an emergent culture which accepted and acknowledged the past, whilst attempting to challenge and meet the demands and potential of the future. Developing from previous decades, the 1990s reflected nostalgically, at times, whilst embracing new digital and micro-technologies with aplomb. The technological revolution, specifically, in relation to personal mobile innovations such as the mobile phone, lap-top computers, and portable music systems, created a near nomadic and individualistic population, who could move, work and communicate wherever they were. The distance between man and machine was lessening. Conversely, but as an extension of this new sense of the individual, more hedonistic desires emerged, which embraced and re-appropriated the past in new forms, embracing the decorative and the possibilities of the imagination. One might see this as a pre-millennium malaise, a correlation of fear and enthusiasm for the *fin de siècle* – change was imminent.

In Britain, 1988 was designated the 'second summer of love', in which Acid House dance music and the associated rave culture dominated popular culture. Taking reference from the hippie movement of the 1960s, Acid House was a rebellious form of hedonism, marked in terms of fashion borrowed readily from the

OPPOSITE PAGE **1990S**
Detail of a floral printed polyester mix shift dress by SupaStyles, originally made in the early 1960s, but sold and worn as vintage clothing in the late 1990s.
Private collection

late 1960s. Acid House fused music styles – compiled by a DJ – cultural references and motifs, whilst resurrecting psychedelia in stylistic form, with large flowers in acid colours.[31] Emerging from street culture, it lacked the professionalism in design associated with established fashion manufacturers and, as a consequence, prints were often hastily transferred on to ready-made garments to create club/rave-wear which could be combined with vintage and shop-bought goods. New technology and increased access to home computers allowed the development of such a DIY home-print culture to emerge and to turn around so quickly. Similarly, young designers, as a legacy of 1980s design and enterprise, and urban regeneration initiatives were able to set up small businesses servicing the needs of young 'ravers'. This was certainly the case in Afflecks Palace in Manchester, where ready-made and hand-made, hand-printed garments were sold alongside boldly patterned vintage items, suitable not just for clubbing, but day-wear as well. Such styles were quickly adopted into the mainstream, and high street shops started to stock bold, brightly coloured patterns.

Acid House certainly fuelled a nostalgia for what was perceived as the innocence of the 1960s and 1970s, with the smiley faced references to drug culture often mis-represented as a sign of childhood and naivety, of times past and lost. Certainly, the early years of the decade were marked with the onslaught of de-industrialisation, unemployment and free-market capitalism, which encouraged a rebellious and hedonistic backlash that referenced a time before the all-pervasive influence of Thatcherism.

The final decade of the 20th century marked an era of tentative faith in the future; in 1990 Margaret Thatcher resigned as Prime Minister and by 1997 Thatcherism appeared to be at an end, with a new Labour Government elected under the slogan 'Things can only get better'. The initial phase of the new administration signalled a new mood of the times, a more youthful approach to social organisation, which was to become a sign of progressive optimism.

The 1990s marked a distinct change in textiles technology, which enabled fabrics to not just be understood as a flat surface, but also as a three-dimensional object. New techniques embraced fabric as sculptural, and heat-transfer printing encouraged designers to experiment with form and print simultaneously. This meant that shape came not merely from construction technique and clever cutting, but from the moulding of fabrics. The potential of cloth was now being explored and developed in unprecedented ways; rather than the traditional understanding of fabric as a surface in need of decoration, it was a vehicle to express movement with more than one dimension. These explorations into shape, form and surface were not limited to print, but involved a variety of new mechanised techniques such as laser cutting and layering, which allowed fabrics to reveal areas previously hidden, and be modelled into new forms.

31   Sean O'Hagan, 'Fifty Years of Pop', *The Observer*, 2 May 2004

This era marked the digital age, a flat screen with multi-dimensional possibilities, mutable and endless, which encouraged new approaches to an understanding of fabric and print. Computer technology enabled designers to move away from drawing boards and realise more innovative forms of design, exploring the use of photography, scale, and shape. Computer Aided Design encouraged innovation through the use of technology, but also enabled designers to think outside the frame; in some cases this meant that a silk-screen was no longer a flat surface, but could be built into a solid form with the addition of found objects to create pattern, or removed completely to create textiles with no solid form at all. This potential was explored in interior design and art textiles through 'virtual' textiles, which created an essence of fabric, projected on to a designated space to express mood, i.e. Anke Jacob, or to evoke a sense of touch in an impersonal world, i.e. Lia Cook. In relation to fashion prints, technology explored the meaning of hand-produced work in the digital age, and prints expressed the seeming invisibility of the maker/designer, with fabric exhibiting near transparent patterns.

Similarly, fashion design recognised the possibilities of virtual technology, with designers such as Pia Myrvold, creating 'cyber-couture' collections, which encourage consumers to interact digitally with the design process.[32]

As with all eras, no one style or technique can be seen as all-embracing, and although one might assume that a fondness and reliance on technology exemplifies a society willing to emulate Lyotard's realm of the post-human,[33] technology was still viewed by some with suspicion. A growing concern regarding the environment, emerging as a result of increased globalisation, the pre-eminence of multi-national corporations and Green politics created experimental possibilities in textile design. Investigation into the production and growth of organic fibres coincided with research into ethical and environmentally friendly dyeing and printing. This often involved a re-evaluation of traditional processes and techniques, mirroring much earlier examples, i.e. the Arts and Crafts Movement.

So, whilst there was a distinct move towards and against technology as a form of inspiration and manufacture, there also was some middle ground, which followed a more traditional design route, whilst developing from post-modern sensibilities from the previous decade. This took the form of fusion and expansion, perhaps a more philosophical approach to pattern rather than fabric, which looked at the motif and repeat, aiming to express new surface decorations. An example of this approach to pattern creation can be seen in the work of design duo Eley Kishimoto,[34] who fused traditional motifs with edgy styling, for both fashion and interiors. The fusion of the old and new, and east and west, exemplified a post-modern appreciation of techniques and pattern.[35]

32 Bradley Quinn, *Techno Fashion*, Berg, 2002
33 Jean-François Lyotard, *The Postmodern Condition: A Report on Knowledge*, Manchester University Press, 1984
34 *Pattern Crazy*, exhibition curated by Carol McNicoll and Jacqui Poncelet, at the Crafts Council, July-September 2002.
35 Lesley Jackson, *20th Century Pattern Design*, Mitchell Beazley, 2002, pp.110-115

'It was a long strappy summer dress with a floral print of red and pink roses featuring specks of light green foliage. It had side ties that I tied at the back which gave it a nipped-in waist and the skirt was kind of A-line. I wore it teamed with a rather lovely army (sludge-coloured) green vest and Doc Marten boots–what an ensemble!'

OPPOSITE PAGE **1950s**
Detail of a vintage floral printed
cotton dress.
Private collection

The juxtaposition of seemingly opposite ideas, signs and motifs, was also evident in popular culture, and certainly in relation to the re-appropriation of the floral printed dress by young women during the period.[36] Historically linked to notions of femininity, young women interviewed outlined how floral printed dresses showed their allegiance to a masculine grunge/rock culture, whilst expressing a new femininity associated with new media role models, including actresses Alicia Silverstone and Liv Tyler. For interviewees, fashion inspiration came from the media rather than couture houses, and as a result fashion was about performativity and an expression of the self as 'cool' rather than 'fashionable'. Indeed, fashion, it appeared, was something they didn't want to be associated with; something that was for older and less expressive people.

For interviewees who were teenagers in the 1990s, floral print dresses were described as subversive, exemplifying the opportunity to express an anti-respectability, which was both mainstream and individual. They represented the potential for re-appropriation, manipulation through customisation and accessorisation and the potential to emulate the styles of their media and fashion role models.[37]

> 'I do remember one floral dress. I bought it when grunge was fashionable and I was madly in love with Kurt Cobain in an attempt to be cool. It was a long strappy summer dress with a floral print of red and pink roses featuring specks of light green foliage. It had side ties that I tied at the back which gave it a nipped in waist and the skirt was kind of A-line. I wore it teamed with a rather lovely army (sludge coloured) green vest and Doc Marten boots – what an ensemble! I bought it in Top Shop and I think it cost between £20-£30. I absolutely loved that dress and when I wore it I felt incredibly cool – the bees knees – when in fact, on reflection, I probably looked a right idiot! I was trying to emulate the style of Alicia Silverstone in the Aerosmith videos of the time (I believe 'Crazy' was one of them). I think she wore a short floral dress in one of the videos with a pair of scuffed DMs. I remember my mum commented that she liked the dress but wished I would wear it with a nice pair of sandals rather than "those unflattering boots".[38]

The rejection of the respondent's mother as a role model in favour of the then teen celebrity Alicia Silverstone, combined with a quest for 'coolness' highlights a transition from familial to collective role models based on age and peer group. Indeed, the creation of 'cool' was not a response to the dictates of the fashion industry, but a personal manipulation and interpretation of existing styles to create an individual 'whole'.

The distinction between what was considered fashionable and what was 'cool' recurred in the testimonies. 'Cool', it appeared, was a personal response to 'fashionable' mass market clothing, available to the teenagers on small budgets. It was about making something everyone else had your own.

> 'I had a great brown floral dress, which is a bit of a contradiction I

36 An oral history project was undertaken with a group of young women who were teenagers in the 1990s and their responses to floral frocks were recorded.

37 Recent studies on consumerism have outlined the significance of what happens to clothes once they leave the shop. The findings from these studies have highlighted that the consumption of goods offers consumers more freedom, pleasure and power, as they can be appropriated and re-appropriated to suit individual needs and wants. See A McRobbie, *In the Culture Society*, London: Routledge, 1999, p.34

38 Zoe interviewed December 2004

suppose, you don't normally buy a pretty floral dress in BROWN, but it was fake 60s style flower power print that I bought when I was about 14 and wore (constantly) until I was about 18, it was stretchy lycra type fabric but not tight, not too short. Just right. It probably only cost a tenner and I altered it on a sewing machine myself. I suppose it was bought from the only local clothes shop in our town when I was younger, that's now closed. It made me feel summery, not fashionable but that was fine by me. I felt cool and it said a lot about how I was at the time. It was a familiar old thing that I would still wear now if I wasn't two stone heavier and a foot taller.'[39]

The floral, modified dress became a symbol of the individual self, rather than a sign of the 'mass' fashionable self. However, the notion of individuality was extended to include the respondents' peer group through the sharing of clothes, which demonstrates the potential of clothing as a social mediator.

'Me and my friends would all wear it, in fact it did the rounds so much I still have photos of old mates wearing my lovely little dress, including a big group photo of us all on my 18th birthday, with me sporting my old faithful flowery brown dress. I remember one occasion and the embarrassment of having it pulled up around my ears by my best friend when we were out in a busy pub, the next day I got her back when she wore the same dress and I pulled it up around her ears when we were out shopping on a busy high street. Why we always wore the dress I don't know...'.[40]

The dress here represented a bond between individuals that aided a sense of inclusion. Similarly, it represented both good and embarrassing times, of modesty and display, of group and individual identity, of fitting in and (in a somewhat shameful way) of standing out. The emphasis appeared to evoke a sense of fun, femininity on one's own terms, and therefore can be seen as the expression of new found freedom.

The 1990s can be assessed as a period of tentative transition: the rejection of the past, whilst maintaining contact with it through traditional references and motifs, which could be appropriated and subverted as required. The impact of new technologies enhanced the potential for textile development, as well as new approaches and responses to floral prints. Similarly, the young women interviewed still wanted to find 'love' as women in the past had, but they were able to address issues of femininity through the media and their peer groups, rather than emulating older women and traditional modes of fashionability. Indeed, youth culture and experimentation typified the era, not necessarily in revolutionary terms as had been the case in previous decades, as it embraced, manipulated and added to mass manufactured high street goods. Equally, new technology didn't really result in new products; it extended and questioned existing boundaries, taking fashion and textiles to multi-dimensional levels which could be interpreted by consumers in a variety of different ways.

39 Julie interviewed December 2004
40 Julie interviewed December 2004

Conclusion

The history of the 20th century can also be seen as the history of the floral printed dress (and vice versa). Often, the floral motifs that pattern dresses are also inscribed with cultural and social attitudes of a given time. Therefore they embody Zeitgeist in the same way that fashion does – it talks to a society about itself and acts as a social marker to future generations.

Floral printed dresses are important; not only do they feature in couture collections, worn by models on the catwalk and in the pages of glossy fashion magazines, they have also been wardrobe staples throughout the 20th century for women of any age, commemorated in family photographs. The floral printed dress for this reason is significant; it demonstrates fashion 'in action' or the diffusion of styles, motifs and techniques, as well as suggesting a democratisation of fashion, available to all, regardless of budget. Ultimately, the floral printed dress is both ordinary and extraordinary. It addresses and represents memories, memories of past times, of romances, holidays, people and places. It is an embodiment of the nostalgic. One oral history respondent, Natalie, noted that her grandmother was firmly established in her memory through her penchant for floral dresses:

> 'My grandma was a rather large woman with a big round belly. The dress I'm thinking of stretched tightly across her belly and was in spring colours, actually quite citrus – pink, white and yellow flowers. The print was quite a big design. It came with a matching jacket and finished at her knees. I remember it being that viscose material – maybe a cotton mix – it wasn't a nice material to cuddle her in as it was a bit scratchy. I think she used to buy them from the catalogue. This memory is quite vague but it reminds me of Sunday lunchtimes in the garden waiting for the BBQ food and stuffing myself with crisps and dips when I was about 11.'[41]

The testimony reflects an understanding of family, but also of lineage, of times past and the distance between the here and now and the there and then. References to the fabric and colours of the 'large' design, as well as the mode of purchase, situate the memory in time, but also demonstrate a common recollection of 'what granny wore'. Grandma was not fashionable, but she was a significant character in the life of the respondent and, as a consequence, floral dresses and

41 Natalie, interviewed November 2004

'Granny' became synonymous. Tinged with nostalgia, the comments pay testimony to an understanding of not just 'family times' and the youthful recklessness of 'stuffing' oneself with party food, but of how 'grandma' felt when embraced, and intimates her position within the family, how she was perhaps 'larger than life', so much so that her clothes couldn't contain her.

Nostalgia also emanates from the garments as a result of the prints' reference to the natural world. The notion of the flower as motif has a long symbolic history deriving from a sense of an unchanging past, in which nature is seen as untainted by the onslaught of technological progress, pure and harmonious and almost 'other-worldly'. As a result, natural motifs are seemingly stuck in time, and consequently appear to be outside fashion and the avant-garde. This has certainly been the view of fashion historians. As Marnie Fogg notes in her recent book, *Print in Fashion:*

> *'The appreciation of flowers is part of that universal yearning for a pastoral idyll that evokes the simplicity of a sun-filled childhood spent running through meadows. In the frenetic pace of modern urban life, city dwellers tend to feel progressively more alienated from nature, and so seek solace in a romanticised rural idyll.'* [2]

As Fogg intimates, floral designs certainly become more apparent in fashion at times of social instability, as demonstrated in the 1970s and in the nostalgic yearnings of Liberty's Tana Lawn designs, as well as being the subject of many style revivals, for example Art Nouveau in the late 1960s.

But floral designs can not be merely categorised as stable, unchanging and solely the reflection of a backward looking society. Floral prints neither shy away from technology, nor do they defy the laws of fashion; prints, motifs and their shape and form change in accordance with fashion, and print and fibre technologies enhance and diversify motifs and patterns.

Floral motifs have a particular place within fashion and cultural history. From the smaller motifs of the 1930s through the bolder patterns of the 1950s and on into modern times the floral frock recurs throughout 20th century dress history. Prints, like the dresses they adorn, are fashionable, but more importantly they express the fashionability and personal identity of the wearer.

42 Marnie Fogg, *Print in Fashion*, BT Batsford, 2006, p.27.

Floral motifs have also been associated with notions of the feminine and the construction of femininity. Floral frocks are garments worn almost exclusively by women and as a result the connection appears to be quite obvious. But like the questionable understanding of florals as a sign of an unchanging world, femininity too is an unstable construct, changing and adapting with social conventions and norms. This is most obviously represented in relation to floral printed dresses throughout the 20th century in two ways; firstly as a response to notions of modesty and display, and secondly through the appropriation and re-appropriation of the garments (i.e. the ways in which they are worn and the messages the wearer wants to convey).

Floral Frocks has aimed to establish the significance of floral printed dresses as representative of fashion, as a means of expressing identity, as a way of remembering the past through the objects and photographs of them, and demonstrating the ways in which fashion can be democratized both through the fashion system and as a rejection of it. The clothes we wear are very important. They communicate something about us to others at any given time. Not only do they say something about who we are, or who we would like to be, or how we would like to be seen by others, but they connect us with the contemporary world in which we live. They link us to places, people, times, memories that reach far beyond our wardrobes; they remind us of the naivety of youth, of celebrations, lost friends, family, and experiences that demonstrate our engagement with the Zeitgeist, whether we see ourselves or our clothes as 'fashionable'.

Most women will have owned or known someone who wore a floral printed dress. They are everywhere and have been for a very long time, and therefore we can assume that they are quite ordinary. But because they tend to be worn for 'special' occasions, and because they are associated with holidays, dances and leisure activities, they are much more than mundane. Because 'Granny' wore them, because 'mum' wore them and because we wear them, they become part of our life narratives – and that makes them extra-ordinary.

1930s
A floral frock and a vase of summer flowers.
Fashion Museum

OPPOSITE PAGE **1950s**
Detail of a floral printed rayon shirtwaister.
Private collection

Bibliography

Andrews M *The Acceptable Face of Feminism: the Women's Institute as a Social Movement*, Lawrence and Wishart, 1997

Arnold R *Fashion, Desire and Anxiety*, I B Tauris, 2001

Ash J & Wilson E (eds) *Chic Thrills: A Fashion Reader*, Pandora, 1992

Barr A & York P *The Official Sloane Ranger's Handbook*, Angus Robertson Publishers, 1983

Booker C *The Seventies: Portrait of a Decade*, Allen Lane, 1980

Boydell C *Our Best Dresses: The Story of Horrockses Fashions Limited*, Harris Museum and Art Gallery, Preston, 2001

Boydell C & Schoeser M (eds) *Disentangling Textiles*, Middlesex University Press, 2002

Breward C *The Swinging Sixties*, V&A Publications, 2006

Breward C, Ehrman E, & Evans C *The London Look: Fashion from Street to Catwalk*, Yale University Press, 2004

Burman B (ed) *The Culture of Sewing: Gender, Consumption and Home Dressmaking*, Berg, 1999

Calder A & Sheridan D (eds) *Speak for Yourself: A Mass Observation Anthology*, Jonathan Cape, 1984

Chambers I *Popular Culture: The Metropolitan Experience*, Routledge, 1986

Conran S *Superwoman*, Outlet, 1978

May 1968
Hilary wears a cotton dress with simple stylised flowers bought from a catalogue, such as Kay's or Freemans, for her daughter's christening at Prince's Risborough, Buckinghamshire.
Private collection

OPPOSITE PAGE
A floral frock for a summer photo with the family.
Private collection

De La Haye (ed) *The Cutting Edge: 50 Years of British Fashion*, V&A Publishing, 1996

Donnelly M *Sixties Britain*, Longman, 2005

Fogg M *Boutique: A 60s Cultural Icon*, Mitchell Beazley, 2003

Fogg M *Print in Fashion*, B T Batsford, 2006

Ford B (ed) *Modern Britain*, Cambridge University Press, 1988

Gardiner J *From the Bomb to the Beatles*, Collins & Brown, 1999

Gardiner J *Wartime: Britain 1939-1945*, Headline Review, 2005

Graham T & Blanchard T *Dressing Diana*, Phoenix Illustrated, 1998

Green J *All Dressed Up: The Sixties and the Counter Culture*, Jonathan Cape, 1998

Hall C *Forties in Vogue*, the Condé Nast Publications Ltd, Octopus Books, 1985

Handley S *Nylon: the Manmade Fashion Revolution*, Bloomsbury Publishing plc, 1999

Harris J, Hyde S & Smith G *1966 and all that: Design and the Consumer in Britain 1960-1969*, Trefoil Publications, 1986

Hebdidge D *Subculture: The Meaning of Style*, Routledge, 1979

Hewitt P (ed) *The Sharper World: A Mod Anthology*, Helter Skelter Publishing, 1999

Hinchcliffe F *Thirties Floral Fabrics*, Webb & Bower Michael Joseph, 1988

Hollows J *Feminism, Femininity and Popular Culture*, Manchester University Press, 2000

Hopkins H *The New Look: A Social History of the Forties and Fifties*, Secker and Warburg, 1964

Horwood K *Keeping Up Appearances: Fashion and Class Between the Wars*, Sutton Publishing, 2005

Hulanicki B *From A to Biba*, Hutchinson, 1983

Ikoku I *British Textile Design From 1940 to the Present*, V&A Publishing, 1999

Jackson L *The New Look: Design in the Fifties*, Thames & Hudson, 1991

Jackson L *20th Century Pattern Design*, Mitchell Beazley, 2002

Kawamura K *Fashion-ology: An Introduction to Fashion Studies*, Berg, Oxford, 2005

Kirkham P (ed) *The Gendered Object*, Manchester University Press, 1996

Levy S *Ready, Steady, Go: Swinging London and the Invention of Cool*, Fourth Estate, 2003

Lewis P *The Fifties*, Heinemann, 1978

Lurie A *The Language of Clothes*, Owl, 1981

Lyotard J-F *The Postmodern Condition: A Report on Knowledge*, Manchester University Press, 1984

McDowell C *Forties Fashion and the New Look*, Bloomsbury Publishing plc, 1997

McRobbie A *Postmodernism and Popular Culture*, London: Routlege, 1994

Maitland S (ed) *Very Heaven: Looking Back at the 1960s*, Virago, 1988

Mayer Thurman C C *Textiles in the Art Institute of Chicago*, The Art Institute of Chicago, 1992

Mendes, V & Hinchcliffe, F *Ascher, Fabric Art Fashion*, Victoria and Albert Museum, 1987

Mulvagh J *Vogue History of Twentieth Century Fashion*, Viking, 1988

Munns J & Rajan G (eds) *A Cultural Studies Reader*, Longman, 1995

Nead L *Myths of Sexuality*, Blackwell, 1988

O'Mahony M & Braddock S (eds) *Textiles and New Technology*, Crafts Council, 1994

Parker R & Pollock G *Old Mistresses: Women, Art and Ideology*, Pandora, 1981

Partington A 'The Designer Housewife in the 1950s', in **Attfield J and Kirkham P (eds)**, *A View from the Interior: Women and Design*, The Women's Press, 1989

Quant M *Quant by Quant*, Cassell and Co Ltd, 1966

Quinn B *Techno Fashion*, Berg, 2002

Robinson J *Fashion in the 1930s*, Oresko Books, 1978

Samuel R *Theatres of Memory*, Verso, 1994

Sandbrook D *Never Had it So Good*, Abacus, 2006

Sandbrook D *White Heat: A History of Britain in the Swinging Sixties*, Little Brown, 2006

Segal L & McIntosh M (eds) *Sex Exposed: Sexuality and the Pornography Debate*, London: Virago, 1992

Shoeser M *Fabrics and Wallpapers*, Bell & Hyman, 1986

Sparke P *As Long as it's Pink: The Sexual Politics of Taste*, Pandora, 1995

Steele V *Fifty Years of Fashion: New Look to Now*, Yale University Press, 2000

Stewart R *Design and British Industry*, John Murray, 1991

Thackara J *Design After Modernism*, Thames & Hudson, 1988

Watson, L *Vogue: Twentieth Century Fashion*, Carlton Books, 1999

Whiteley N *Pop Design: From Modernism to Mod*, Design Council, 1989

Wilcox C & Mendes V, *Modern Fashion in Detail*, V&A Publishing, 1991

Wilson E & Taylor L *Through the Looking Glass: A History of Dress from 1860 to the Present Day*, BBC Books, 1989

Woodham J *Twentieth Century Design*, Oxford University Press, 1997

Index

Page numbers in **bold** type refer to illustrations and captions

Acknowledgements

1950s
Floral frocks for a summer day out.
Fashion Museum

Floral Frocks is one of the outcomes of a research project which was initiated by Professor John Miles and Dr Jo Turney at the Bath School of Art and Design, Bath Spa University. The University also supported the project through research funding and as a part of its 'Artswork' scheme.

The book is a partnership between the Bath School of Art and Design and the Antique Collectors' Club, and our thanks to everybody at both organisations who assisted with the preparation and production of *Floral Frocks*.

Floral Frocks was designed by Northbank, Bath. A particular thank you to everybody involved with this aspect of the project.

One of the outcomes of the floral frock research project was an exhibition *Pick of the Bunch – a celebration of the floral frock* at Bath & North East Somerset Council's Fashion Museum in summer 2007. The exhibition concept was developed by Howard Batho and Rosemary Harden at the Fashion Museum.

This book is based on real examples of floral frocks from the 20th century that survive in both museum and private collections in Britain, and which were most generously lent to and included in the exhibition at the Fashion Museum. Thank you to the Fashion Museum in Bath, the Harris Museum and Art Gallery, Preston, the Gallery of Costume in Manchester and the Victoria and Albert Museum in London, and to all the private lenders for their kindness and assistance in enabling these frocks to be included in the project.

We would like to say a particular thank you to the many individuals who have generously shared their family photographs and their memories of wearing floral frocks with us. Their kindness in allowing us to use such personal information helped to define and to shape the floral frocks project, giving it a richness and resonance which we would not otherwise have been able to achieve. Thank you to them all.

In addition to the many family photographs, we have been fortunate in being able to reproduce a number of photographs taken by professional photographers of women wearing floral frocks. Our thanks to Bath & North East Somerset Council, to Condé Nast Publications Ltd, to the Lee Miller Archive, and to the National Portrait Gallery, London for assistance with this.

Every effort has been made to secure permission to reproduce the images contained within this book, and we are grateful to the individuals and institutions who have assisted in this task. Any errors or omissions are entirely unintentional, and the details should be addressed to the publisher.